The Medieval Christmas

Sophie Jackson

SUTTON PUBLISHING

Sutton Publishing Limited
Phoenix Mill · Thrupp · Stroud
Gloucestershire · GL5 2BU

First published 2005

Illustration page i British Library/Bridgeman Art Library; page iii Scala Archives; page iv British Library/Bridgeman Art Library

British Library Cataloguing in Publication Data
A catalogue for this book is available from the British Library.

ISBN 0-7509-4144-8

Typeset in 10/16.5pt Iowan Old Style
Typesetting and origination by
Sutton Publishing Limited.
Printed and bound in England by
J.H. Haynes & Co. Ltd, Sparkford.

CONTENTS

INTRODUCTION

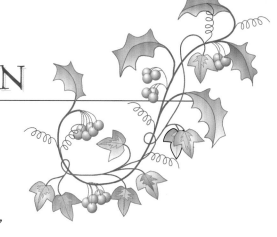

Welcome, sir Christëmas,
Welcome to us all, both more and less
Come near, Nowell!

From a carol attributed to Richard Smart,
Rector of Plymtree, Devon, 1435–77

So entrenched is the view that the modern Christmas has its origins in Victorian times that it comes as a shock to realise that many of the customs we enjoy during the festive season date back to the Middle Ages or earlier. In the medieval period people gave gifts, sang carols, decorated their homes, over-indulged in seasonal food and drink and had their own Father Christmas, known then as St Nicholas. With its lengthy preparations and many saints' days to mark, their Christmas season could last even longer than the modern holiday.

What is more, the medieval Christmas was quite literally a magical time. Most of the important Christmas dates began as powerful pagan celebrations that had been Christianised, although people could not give up the old customs completely and still cast their divination and fertility spells, now using the symbols of Christianity. Lost souls might wander the dark woods, demons might enter the house and cause chaos, but Christmas was the only time when Jesus Christ could also come into every home and drive away the pixies and sprites that threatened to mar the season's joy. The old and the new merged. Saints were honoured in place of the old gods, the old magic became God's miracles and pagan festivals assumed a new life as Christian feasts. The feast of Christmas, with its story of the birth of the Saviour who redeemed mankind from sin and death, was thus harmoniously woven into the fabric of an older tradition, albeit one that still lingered in memories of the past.

A French-influenced fool in his *habit de fou* with bells. *(Bodleian Library, Oxford: MS Laud.lat 114, f. 71)*

When we celebrate Christmas we should remember those joyful medieval festivities. Just as now, so people then would have exchanged gifts, risen early on Christmas Day, gone to church and prepared a feast with roasted birds or boar, spiced alcoholic wassail and rich fruit cakes. They would have played games, often a shade more dangerous than their modern counterparts, danced and sung, and looked forward to the year to come. The medieval Christmas was a lively, vibrant time, eagerly anticipated in the dark months of winter. There were few who did not try and mark it in some way, even the poorest, and incorporating their traditions can serve to enrich our own Christmas.

CHAPTER ONE

MUMMERS, MYSTERIES AND MIRACLES

The History of Mystery and Miracle Plays

The medieval mystery and miracle plays performed at Christmas re-enacted Bible stories and were among some of the most popular entertainments of the Christmas season. They were probably based on an earlier form of religious theatre, the liturgical drama that first appeared in the tenth and eleventh centuries as a means of helping ordinary people learn biblical tales, consisting of very short plays in the vernacular as well as Latin, which gave the common man a chance to understand what was happening.

These early medieval plays were originally performed by monks, but problems soon arose with some of the subjects; for instance, the story of the Massacre of the Innocents posed the question of whether it was right for a monk to represent the evil King Herod. Was it even spiritually sound to portray such a vile act within the walls of a church? The liturgical dramas never went further than the original few short lines, but they served to open up a whole new dimension of entertainment. Secular performers had already started to develop new plays and so the atmosphere was ripe for the mystery and miracle plays to flourish.

As far as we know, the oldest such play was written by Abbot Geoffrey of St Albans in 1110. Taking St Katherine as its subject, it was performed in Dunstable, where the Abbot taught. In the years that followed, many mystery and miracle plays were created and eventually the whole story of the Bible,

from the Creation to Christ's crucifixion and resurrection, and finally Doomsday, were enacted.

The difference between the two types of play was that the mysteries described the stories of the Old and New Testaments, including those of Cain and Abel, Noah's flood, and the Nativity. The miracles, on the other hand, told of the lives of the saints. The miracle plays could be performed in conjunction with the mysteries or as separate short pieces, as was the case with the one about St Katharine.

Pageants

The mystery plays were gathered together in cycles, which related the whole of the Bible. The entire cycle was performed in one day, usually close to Christmas or around Easter, the two most important Christian dates in the Church calendar. At Christmas time they brought life to the dark nights of winter and helped celebrate the festival.

The plays were originally performed in churchyards and large groups of people would gather outside the church to watch. But the actors tended to get carried away and the plays became coarser, ribald and in some parts lewd. In the thirteenth century many of the clergy were no longer prepared to tolerate what they saw as a debasing of the scriptural message and the plays moved out of the churchyards and into the streets.

The actors now had no stage, but that did not stop them. They constructed two-tier wagons called pageants that could be transported to a given place in the town or city, the two levels of the stage providing performance space, with the ground in front of the wagon forming a third stage. Each Bible story had its own scenery and this was fixed to the wagon. In cities such as Chester and York each city guild created a pageant and acted out one Bible story on their own wagon. Thus it was even more important for the plays to be staged on pageants so they could process through the streets, stopping

Music enlivened the dark nights of winter, with bagpipes, recorder and drums among the instruments. (*Bodleian Library, University of Oxford. MS Douce, 18, f. 113v*)

at a designated place, performing their story and then moving on so that the next wagon could take their place and its occupants perform their own play.

The place where the wagons stopped often depended on who could pay the most for the privilege of having the actors perform outside their house. The wealthier merchants and townspeople preferred to watch the plays from the comfort of their homes, and considering how long the cycle could last this is hardly surprising. In York the plays started at four thirty in the morning and did not finish until dusk. Those who could not afford to purchase the privilege of having a performance outside their homes would have to stand in the streets and watch, a brave act in the middle of winter.

The Actors

In liturgical dramas monks had acted out the Bible stories; in the mystery and miracle plays secular players took the roles and performed on the pageants. Any group of people might come together to organise a play for Christmas but in the cities the guilds took over the running of the performances. The large guilds could afford to put on bigger and grander shows because they taxed their members. This tax was used to cover the costs of scenery, costumes and, in some cases, the hiring of the actors, though in other guilds the members took the roles. Actors were paid for performing, though deductions were made for poor acting or forgetting lines.

Despite the guilds' involvement in the plays there was still a stigma attached to entertainers. Though some exceptions were known, most actors were considered the lowest level of society, little better than beggars, cripples or vagabonds. Though this attitude had softened somewhat by the thirteenth century, acting was not considered an honorable occupation and, despite having its own liturgical dramas, the Church frowned upon it. Monks and members of the clergy were strictly forbidden to take part in any of the plays enacted in streets or houses during festivals. Those who were found doing so were punished.

The actors were mainly amateurs but threw themselves into their parts. When Father Nicholas de Neuchâtel-en-Lorraine played Christ in Metz, France, in 1437, he almost died on the cross.

There was often little money, unless the guilds supplied the funds, and the players often performed in their everyday clothes. Such costumes as there were would most likely have been based on the fashions of the time, though some characters, such as God, would have required special robes and a mask. The modern York plays are performed in fourteenth-century costume to be in keeping with the original actors' dress.

The York Cycle is but one example of medieval mystery plays. In total forty-eight plays were performed during the cycle, originally acted by different guilds. Imagine all these plays being performed one after another on huge wagons adorned with scenery and actors in fancy costume – it must have been an extraordinary sight and one that kept the audience enthralled the entire day. The pageant wagons were housed on Pageant Green, though they no longer are. On a day near Christmas the great wagons were drawn by horses away from the Green and rumbled through the city, making twelve stops at each of which the actors performed their short plays.

Outside the cities few would have known much about the elaborate mystery cycles unless they happened to have visited a place where they were being performed. For poorer villages and hamlets another form of entertainment enlivened the dark winter. It was less expensive and did not require vast stages or a whole day to perform. This less grand form of acting had its own class of actors, the mummers, and was very different from the mystery plays of York and Chester.

Mumming

Mumming is an ancient form of street theatre. The practice began in Britain before the coming of Christianity and was a fertility rite marking the death of the summer during winter and its rebirth in the spring. The word 'mumming' or 'mummers' (meaning the performers) is controversial in origin. There are two possible explanations. It may derive from the German word *Mumme* which means mask or masker, suggesting the word did not come into use in England until after the Germanic tribes invaded in the fifth century and that before this the players would have had another name. The other theory is that the word comes from the Greek *momme*, meaning frightening mask or ogress. Both names refer to the masks the mummers wore to disguise themselves during a performance. This disguise was important for it was believed that if a mummer was recognised, the magic of the ritual would be broken and might even prevent the sun from returning. In some places it is still important that mummers are not recognised while performing their plays.

Because of the timing of the ancient ceremony, in mid-winter when the days were at their shortest

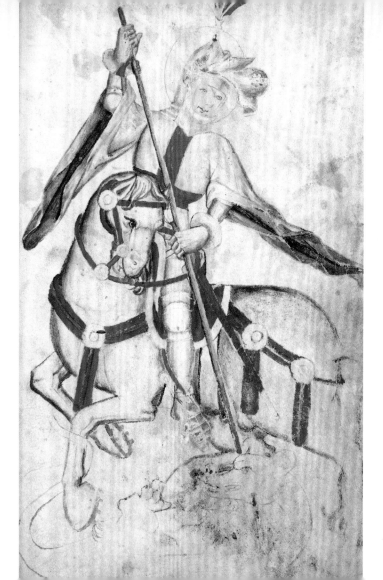

St George slaying the dragon, a common theme in mummers' plays. *(Bodleian Library, University of Oxford. MS Don. d.85, fol.130r)*

and the sun's rays weak, mumming has become associated with Christmas. The medieval mummers would start their performances around Halloween and continue through to Easter. The association with Christmas happened when Christianity reached Britain and pagan ritual and practice were given new meanings that fitted into a Christian context and were assimilated into the new religion. So the popular ancient rituals of mumming that enacted the death of the sun and its rebirth in the spring were retained.

By the Middle Ages mumming activities had already lost some of their original significance. People were no longer as afraid as their primitive ancestors had been that the sun would not return, though they still continued the old practices just to be certain. The mummers were turning into actors, their performances now as much for entertainment as to follow ancient ritual. The Anglo-Saxons might have used some of the mumming rituals as training for their warriors, but as the medieval period progressed, so gradually mumming became solely a Christmas entertainment and its original purpose and meaning were obscured.

Medieval Christianity brought new characters to the mummers' plays. Of these, Beelzebub was the most common and he frequents most modern versions of the old plays. There was also Father Christmas or, as he was sometimes known in medieval times, Old Man Winter, who would appear wielding a club and shouting – certainly not a Father Christmas we would recognise. The most important new character, who transformed the part of the hero and altered the nature of some of the mumming, was St George. He came to fame after supposedly killing a dragon in Egypt around the third century and his life was described in a book entitled *Famous Historie of the Severn Champions of Christendom* that included six other champions. St George became a staple of medieval mumming plays, sometimes accompanied by his dragon, though this was a difficult and expensive prop to make, hence the dragon became more symbolic and his place was taken by other villains. After the crusades this became the Turkish Knight.

St George was eventually replaced in later periods by Prince George or King George, but his Christian influence on the art of the mummers was not forgotten and in modern mumming St George is beginning to reappear.

The Three Types of Mummers' Plays

There are several different forms of mummers' plays, but not all performers who went under the name of mummers actually acted. Some simply cavorted about the streets in animal masks, occasionally singing carols and often visiting houses to collect money or a drink of ale. These performers could be little more than beggars and sometimes trouble makers. The true mummers performed three types of mummers' plays which were the Hero/Combat, The Wooing Ceremony and The Sword Dance. All treat the themes of death and rebirth, each in a different way, and to understand the mummers it is necessary to understand the differences between their plays.

The Hero/Combat plays are the best known. The mummers stand in a circle in the middle of their audience and proceed to speak lines which are rhymed. They start with the prologue, introducing the characters who are about to perform. (The main mummer, such as St George, may read this piece and step forward as he does so.) Though the actors usually form a circle, some of the plays contain directions for entrances and exits just as for a play performed on a stage in a theatre. In this case, as the introduction is spoken the main characters join the speaker in readiness to perform. After the prologue the hero often speaks, his speech usually making little sense other than to act as a challenge to his opponent, the villain. This villain can be any character – in the case of St George it could be a symbolic dragon or the Turkish Knight.

The challenges result in a sword fight. This can be highly ritualised, like the Sword Dance Ceremony, but always ends in the death of one of the combatants, as often the hero as the villain. Then follows the lament, performed by either the hero or another character. The lamenter regrets the death of the combatant and calls urgently for a doctor to come and revive the fallen man. A quack doctor then appears and attempts to resuscitate the dead man in a scene that is comic and often forms the main part of the play. Before his cure is even carried out the doctor recites a list of the diseases he has cured, the places he has been and in general blows his own trumpet in a long speech before he finally produces a bottle of medicine which he gives to the corpse. Miraculously the strange potion revives the fallen man. But this is not the end of the play. Occasionally there is another fight, sometimes with different combatants and if one dies he may not be revived as before. The play concludes with the arrival of superfluous characters who appear to have no real function in the plot but have nevertheless become a part of the ritual. Most common among these late arrivals is Beelzebub. He appears just in time for the ending of the play with a seasonal song.

The Wooing Ceremony is similar to the Hero/ Combat in that it too has rhymed speeches and a death and revival scene. However, the story, in as

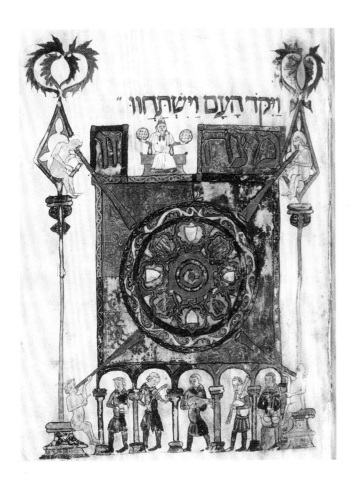

Musicians playing a selection of instruments from the Barcelona Haggadah, a magnificent illuminated Hebrew manuscript from the middle of the fourteenth century. (*British Library, MS Add. 14761 fol. 61r.*)

much as there is one, is very different. The play has two versions, one, known as the Recruiting Sergeant play, has a love triangle as its theme. A farm labourer is courting a lady but when he joins the army he abandons his love and she transfers her affections to the character known as the Fool, marrying him instead. There follows a scene with an Old Dame and the ever-popular Beelzebub. They argue and Beelzebub knocks down the Old Dame, killing her. Once again the doctor is summoned, this time to cure the Old Woman, which he proceeds to do in a comic scene.

The second version of the drama, is known as the Wooing Ceremony, in this case several suitors court the same lady and try to win her hand. There may be fighting among these suitors and the doctor has to be summoned to revive those who die. When none of the suitors succeeds in convincing the lady to marry, she instead falls in love with the Fool. The play then proceeds as before.

The Sword Dance differs from the previous plays in that it has little acting, though rhymed lines are spoken. Instead, it revolves around the sword dance. There are two separate categories of sword dance that are unique to certain areas of Britain. Durham and Northumberland have the Rapper dance, while Yorkshire and South Durham have the Long Sword dance. Both involve forming a circle while the mummers grasp their neighbours' swords, forming a rigid ring during the Long Sword dance, but a moveable ring during the Rapper dance.

The dance begins with the leader of the mummers, who sings an introduction, naming the performers individually. He walks in a circle followed by the men, as he names them, until his song is finished and the mummers form a circle each holding his neighbour's sword. The dance begins with the men jumping over or dancing under the held swords, never letting go their grip. They dance around and weave through the swords until a pattern is formed with the weapons, usually representing a five-pointed star in the middle, depending on the number of dancers. The name of this linkage of swords can be star, rose, nut or lock. The shape is displayed to the audience, the mummers moving round in a circle, the swords above their heads. At a given point another mummer enters the ring and the knot of swords is placed over his head and around his neck. The dancers then move in unison to lift the swords back over his head. Sometimes the trapped mummer wears a hat that is removed during this process. When the swords are removed the mummer is 'killed' and then a doctor is called upon to revive him. This final enactment of trapping the mummer occurs only in the Long Sword dance, where the blades are actually made of wood and it is quite safe for the mummer to put his head in the knot. The Rapper dance, which dates from much later, uses blades of sprung steel which are deadly sharp and often only the mummer's hat is trapped in these dances.

Sword dances were essential to the mummers' plays and a part of the popular medieval Christmas traditions. They formed, with the other two types, an integral part of the seasonal festivities and one that carries on to this day.

The Mummers and their Disguises

In pre-Christian times it was imperative that the mummers could not be identified. They would blacken their faces and possibly put on simple masks or the fringed caps that were later used in medieval mummery. The disguise was needed so that ordinary men could be transformed into magicians capable of summoning back the sun for another year. The magic could be broken if anyone called out to someone they recognised: the spell would fail and the sun would not return. As time went on, the earlier perceived danger that lay in revealing a dancer's identity diminished. It was still considered bad manners for a person to make it known that they recognised a mummer and the performers still wore their costumes, but it was now for the sake of maintaining the mystery of the performance and not to enact an ancient rite.

The evidence for medieval mumming costumes is limited. Perhaps one of the simplest would have been a tall headdress from which rags or ribbons were suspended so as to conceal the face. This would form a fringe around the head and might hang in tiers. The medieval mummers would have used old clothes worn beyond repair and other ragged items that could be cut into strips and sewn to a cone or cap on the head. They might also have attached knots or rosettes to their clothes and they would still have blackened their faces to heighten their disguise.

Manuscript evidence shows more elaborate costumes. One from the Bodleian Library depicts mummers with animal heads of various kinds, including a stag, hare and wolf. These must have been for courtly performances where there was money to buy the elaborate masks needed to create these effects. What relevance the animal heads had to the performance is unclear, though if one had been a dragon that would have made sense if St George was the hero. Perhaps they were not used for the plays at all but were outfits that cavorting mummers wore as they sang and danced down the streets, knocking on doors and receiving money or a drink for their efforts.

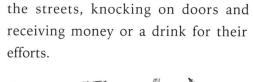

Three mummers wearing animal masks (a stag, a hare and a wolf) dance to the music of a cittern. (*Bodleian Library, University of Oxford. MS Bodleian 264, f. 21v*)

A Modern Mummers' Play

This is a modern adaptation of a mummers' Hero/Combat performance from a play written down in a chapbook in the early eighteenth century. It should last about five minutes, depending on the length of the fight scenes, and is adapted for three people.

Cast:

St George (Prologue and fight scenes)

Dragon (Fight scenes)

Doctor (Revival scenes)

Additional character if desired:

King (Lamenter instead of St George)

The Play:

> *Actors enter and form a semi-circle.*
>
> *St George steps forward.*

ST GEORGE: Silence, hast thou come to see our glory?

My name is George and I have come to sing our story;

Two good fellows I have brought with me,

For to my song they are the key,

First the doctor, good soul and wise,

Here to make a dead man rise,

Then the dragon from land afar,

Come here to sport with me and spar,

Now let our pastime start and hear me relate,

A tale of an older age and date.

I am St George a hero of men and champion brave,

For with my lance in Egypt did I send such a dragon to his

   grave,

And won the hand of the king's daughter,

For my good work and the monster's slaughter,

But I was a prisoner bound not long after,

Until my escape and freedom thereafter.

DRAGON: Hold thy tongue and use your eyes,
See who it is that they do spy,
I am the beast that will be your undoing,
On your guard, your trouble is brewing,
I shall send thee to Satan when you die,
Cut up so small you'll make a mince pie,
Hold I say, for today one must die,
Fight me now, for I know it won't be I,
You shall expire on this pitiful day,
Come draw your sword, fight I say!

St George and the Dragon now fight. Take care with this part and rehearse before the performance, preferably remembering your moves so you know who is going to strike when. Use swords cut from cardboard or buy toy wooden or plastic swords, but do take care and do not use real or imitation blades. At the end of the fight the Dragon dies, though you could alter it so George is killed instead.

Mummers by Jehan de Grise, 1344. Detail from *Romans d'Alexandre*. *(Bodleian Library, University of Oxford. MS Bodley 264, f. 84v)*

ST GEORGE: So noble and brave a foe,

His challenge I heard but now I sorrow,

For he is dead at my sword,

An end dire for the monsters' lord,

I cannot see him lie there dead for sure,

Doctor come forward, bring him your cure.

DOCTOR: My liege I come forward to bring my cure,

And do the bidding of a heart so pure,

As to resurrect this villain here,

To keep your conscience clear.

ST GEORGE: What diseases can he cure?

DOCTOR: Surely I can cure the pox, the palsy, the cold, the fever,

One of my medicines will cure either,

For the coward I can give him courage,

Make him a solider and to war encourage,

For the miser I can break his stronghold,

St George, the king's daughter and the Dragon.

(*Bibliothèque Nationale, Paris, MS Lat.17294, fol. 448*)

Make him used to spending bold,

For the broken arm, leg or head,

I have ointments and poultices to keep the patient out of bed,

Few doctors can rival my skill,

To cure all things that make you ill,

For I have travelled far and wide,

Collecting wisdom to use with pride,

So with this potion I will wake,

The Dragon for St George's sake.

Administers potion.

The Dragon arises.

DRAGON: Horror and bile, was I not slain,

Was the culprit not the true villain?

ST GEORGE: Call me not such for it was I who saved you,

Called this good doctor and made him revive you,

Stand now thy knave,

Or are you not brave,

Face me again for this anger you've brought,

A friend of you I need naught.

DRAGON: A wily fool you be,

To face again a champion such as me.

ST GEORGE: A fool, sir! An insult so vulgar I cannot bear,

Stand before me and face me here,

Name a place, a date, a time,

And I shall be there on the chime.

DRAGON: I shall fight you at the dawn,

I'll meet you there with swords drawn.

ST GEORGE: A coward but delays the fight,

Spar with me now and show your might,

I cannot wait another day,

To pace myself until I can slay,

You, and watch you die,

And leave you on the grass to lie.

DRAGON: Draw your sword and prepare to lose.

ST GEORGE: No more will I take your abuse.

The Dragon and St George fight again; the Dragon is slain.
Alternatively, introduce the King and give him St George's lines,
then he fights the Dragon and either of the two may die.

ST GEORGE: The beast is dead and this time no cure,

He is dead of that I shall ensure,

Carry him away on bearers strong,

And bury him in the ground where he does belong.

The conclusion:

ST GEORGE: This season comes but once a year,

And with it comes what we hold dear,

Merriment and laughter,

Joy from now and hereafter,

With this comes our entertainment,

I hope our play has brought amusement,

Our small troupe has done our best,

But it is not time yet to go and rest.

End with a Christmas carol of your choice.

St George in battle, from the Valencia altarpiece.

(Victoria and Albert Museum, London)

CHAPTER TWO

WILD BOAR AND WASSAIL

edieval Christmas fare was far from plain and boring. As a time of feasting and rejoicing, Christmas was perhaps the only opportunity during the year for peasants to enjoy a satisfying meal that included meat and sweet dishes. There was drinking and singing, ceremonies and games – a chance to overindulge and have fun. The early Church did not approve as it was too much like the pagan Saturn-alia and it was thought that Christians should not behave in such a reckless and gluttonous way. But the feasts and fun continued, with luxurious dishes not usually seen and more than enough to satisfy even the heartiest appetite. Just as now, Christmas dinner was a meal to be remembered.

A grand feast is served. Many dishes sit on the table as the servants bring in more food. Add. MS 42130. Luttrell Psalter, f.280 and f.207v, page 21. (© The British Library)

The Story of the Mince Pie

Modern mince pies are far removed from the original dish. The medieval mince pie was known simply as the Christmas pie (later 'minced' or 'shredded' pie) and contained all types of meat – beef, lamb, goose, chicken – as well as suet, spices and fruit, depending on what was available. And it was not, as now, an after-dinner treat but part of the main meal. It would only be prepared around midwinter and often contained the less choice cuts of meat. It was a dish of left-overs, made with what was left from the winter slaughter of animals. So the combination of meats is not surprising since anything and everything was used to fill up the pie. Suet held the minced meats together and the dried fruit was a common addition to meat pies, giving them a sweetness that was pleasing to the medieval palate.

The use of spices had a social and a symbolic purpose. The spices represented the three gifts the Magi or wise men presented to the baby Jesus: frankincense, myrrh and gold. Gold, though not a fragrant substance like the other two, was treated as a condiment and would also have been present in the later gilded decoration of the pie. The spices had another important purpose, one which we have probably lost sight of today. The use of exotic spices from far-off lands was a sign of luxury and extravagance and an indication of the wealth of the household, as well as showing that this was a very special dish.

We would recognise the pastry of this savoury pie, though the flours used might not always bear a close resemblance to modern varieties. Fine flour for pastry-making was usually only available in wealthier households where the numbers of servants meant there was time to grind and sieve the grain. Poorer people probably had to forgo pastry altogether and make do with a type of unleavened bread full of impurities. Even with the advent of water mills in the seventh century they were mainly associated with high status sites, so it still took many years before a peasant would have been able to make a decent Christmas pie.

Once the pastry was made and fitted into a dish, the meats were added in layers with fruits and spices. The pie would have been large and grand, sometimes left open to display the contents, though more often it was sealed with a lid. It was usually oval in shape and easily transformed into a crib with a tiny pastry baby Jesus sculpted and set on top. It was thought unlucky to cut the pie with a knife – rather like cutting through a real child's crib – so a spoon or the hands were used instead. The first bite was traditionally given to the youngest child present, who could make a wish as he or she tasted the sweetened meats.

The Christmas pie was eaten as part of the feast until the seventeenth century, when Puritans tried to curtail Christmas celebrations. They disapproved of the very idea of pies in the form of a crib and gradually both the shape and the name changed to avoid any links with the old traditions. The Christmas pie became the minced pie, later mince pie, and was made into smaller pies with no baby Jesus.

Yet the old customs still lingered, in particular two customs that have stubbornly refused to die out. The first was widespread across England and was used to ensure good fortune in the coming year. One mince pie is be eaten on each of the twelve days of Christmas, but every pie must be consumed in a different house, a practice that is supposed to ensure good luck for the next twelve months. The second superstition is easier on the stomach. In this case one wish is granted after a person takes the first bite of the first mince pie of Christmas; refusing the pie brings bad luck.

By the late nineteenth century the mince pie had been transformed. With better storage it was no longer necessary for waste meat to be piled into one last, large pie before it rotted too far to be edible. The meat was removed though the suet remains to fix the mincemeat together and most of the spices were left off the list of ingredients, leaving the rich fruits and plenty of added sugar. No longer the main dish of the feast, the mince pie had become an after-dinner treat and so it has remained.

Servants cooking in the open air. Much preparation went into the Christmas feast. (*Bodleian Library, University of Oxford. MS 264, pt 1, f. 170v*)

A Medieval Christmas Pie

FOR THE PASTRY

450g/1lb plain flour
225g/ 8oz suet
Pinch of salt

FOR THE FILLING

225g/8oz mixed minced meat
   (beef, pork and lamb)
1 small onion chopped
1 carrot chopped
2 big cloves of garlic
2 tablespoons mixed fruit
2 tablespoons brown sugar
2 tablespoons red wine
1 tablespoon chopped coriander
1 tablespoon chopped ginger
1½ teaspoons cumin
1½ teaspoons cinnamon
   salt and pepper

1. Place the suet in a saucepan with a covering of water. Put on a high heat and bring to the boil. Remove from the heat and add the flour and salt. Mix together well to form dough. Leave to cool but make sure it does not dry out; if this occurs, add more water in small quantities.

2. Once cool enough to handle, roll out the pastry. Use cutters of two sizes to cut out bases and lids for the pies (depending on the size of the cutters you will get different quantities of pies). This recipe uses one 8cm/3¼in round cutter for the base and one 6cm/2½in round cutter for the lid. Different shapes could be used to create unusual lids, such as star shaped ones. Grease and flour baking tins for small pies and fit the bases into them. If making a large mince pie use a shallow oval dish and line with pastry.

3. Mix together the pork, beef and lamb so you have a quantity of minced meat weighing 225g/½lb. Add to this the chopped coriander, ginger and garlic and mix together thoroughly. At the same time combine the brown sugar, cumin, salt and pepper and cinnamon.

4. Layer the ingredients into the pastry cases. Start with a layer of the meat mixture then add the mixed fruit, onion, carrot and the sugar mixture. Spread the filling evenly between the pies without overfilling them and then pour a teaspoon of wine over each one.

5. Wet the edges of the cases with cold water and fit the tops, gently pushing them into place. Make a hole in the top and brush the lids of the pies with beaten egg.

6. Bake in a preheated oven 220°/fan 195°C/gas mark 6 for between 20 and 25 minutes or until golden brown. Serve warm.

Variation

For a slightly different version prepare the same meat mixture with coriander, ginger and garlic, but then layer that with 2 tablespoons of mixed fruit, 2 tablespoons of red wine and 3 tablespoons of red Leicester cheese. (This is an updated version of the original Christmas pie, based on a recipe by the WDA Food Directorate and used with their kind permission.)

The Boar's Head

ating a boar's head at Christmas is an ancient tradition first introduced into Britain by the Vikings and Romans. The Vikings killed a boar to sacrifice to their god Frey, after whom the day Friday was named. Swine were the sacred animal of this god and it was important to pay tribute to him on special occasions. The Romans honoured their gods with a similar practice, although their sacrifices were not limited to wild boar.

Sacrificial animals were garlanded with flowers and leaves as they were led to their demise and traditionally the boar's head was brought to the table still decked with the garlands and with an apple in its mouth. The Viking tradition was quickly assimilated into English culture, despite its clearly pagan origins. The early Britons and

A pre-Christmas boar hunt, an activity that was eventually brought to a halt as the creature was hunted to extinction in Britain. From *Les très riches heures du Duc de Berry*, by the Limburg Brothers. (*AKG-Images*)

the Anglo-Saxons already sacrificed animals, oxen in particular, which were always slaughtered in time for a great feast. These pagan customs had gradually been Christianised and instead of the animals being slaughtered for pagan gods they were being sacrificed for the one true God. Incorporating the earlier traditions of the boar's head into Christian practice proved a relatively easy transition and it became a common part of Christmas.

Though many of the wealthy ate boar's head at Christmas it was at Queen's College, Oxford that the delicacy became most famous. A carol was even composed to be sung when the boar's head was brought into the dining hall:

> The boar's head in hand bear I,
> Bedecked with bays and rosemary;
> And I pray you, my masters, be merry,
> *Quo testis in convicio.* [So many as are in the feast]

> *Caput apri defero,* [The boar's head I bring]
> *Reddens laudes Domino.* [Giving praises to God]

> The boar's head as I understand,
> Is the rarest dish in all this land,
> Which thus bedecked with gay garland,
> Let us *servire cantico.* [Serve with a song]

> Our steward hath provided this,
> In honour of the King of bliss,
> Which on this day to be served is,
> *In reginensi atrio.* [In the Queen's hall]

This carol was first printed in 1521 and was probably created some years before. At least three others written in the fifteenth century celebrate the bringing in of the animal's head. What is probably the oldest carol to celebrate the boar goes as follows:

Hey! Hey! Hey! Hey!
The boar his head is armed gay.

The boar his head in hand I bring,
With garland gay in porttoring,
I pray you all with me to sing,
With hey!

Lord, knights, and squires,
Parsons, priests and vicars,
The boar his head is in the first dish,
With hey!

Then comes in the second course with much pride,
The cranes, the herons, the bitterns, by their side,
To partridges and the plovers, the woodcocks, and the
    snipe,
With hey!

Larks in hot show ladies for to pick,
Good drink thereto, luscious and fine,
Drinks of Allemaine, Romnay and wine,
With hey!

Good brewed ale and wine, dare I well say,
The boar his head with mustard armed so gay,
Furmenty for pottage, with venison fine,
And the umbles of the doe and all that ever comes in,
Capons well baked, with the pieces of the roe,
Raisins of currants, with other spices more,
With hey!

The Queen's College tradition of bringing in the boar's head began in 1341 and took place on the last Saturday before Christmas. It is said a young student was walking in Shotover Forest near the College reading a book of Aristotle, when he surprised a boar that attacked him. The student might

Slaughtering a pig in December. From the workshop of Gerart Horenbout and Simon Bening. (MS Add. 24098 f.29v *British Library/ Bridgeman Art Library*)

have met a bloody end as boars are notoriously ferocious, had he not reacted to the attack by shoving the works of Aristotle into the open jaws of the beast and down his throat crying *Græcum est!* which means it is Greek. The boar was thus choked, and for his courage a feast was held in the student's honour, which is supposedly how the tradition started. This does not explain why the boar's head is only paraded in at Christmas, but whatever its true origins the festivity carries on to this day, with the boar's head carol still being sung as the cooked head is brought in.

It was not just the head of the boar that was eaten at Christmas. It was an important animal in winter because the meat from its head and fore-parts could be used to make brawn. Even in medieval times, the brawn was not always rendered from wild boar; tame ones were also brought into a barn or stable around November to be fattened up and slaughtered.

Poultry and Stuffing

Though the North American turkey would not have been on the medieval Christmas menu, many other native British birds were consumed and were brought to the table with all the ceremony of the boar's head. When birds were presented to the diners, it was common for them to be made to look alive, as though they had just been persuaded to sit on the platter to be carried into the feasting-hall. This was achieved by carefully skinning the bird before cooking, as opposed to plucking it. The skinned carcass was roasted over a fire and then replaced in its skin, the cuts being sewn up. The head and neck must have been supported or stuffed in some way to ensure they stood up and to make the bird look as though it was alive.

Several types of wild bird were treated in this way. The swan, which was the preserve of the monarch and his or her court, would have looked stunning with its large wings curving over its back and its regal neck stuffed and made to stay in the typical S shape so often seen on living birds. The peacock, another delicacy for the wealthy though not specifically the king or queen, was presented with its full tail and gilded head crest. Sometimes a wick was fitted into the bird's mouth and set alight, adding drama to the festive meal.

The only problem with eating wild birds is that they could prove disagreeable in taste. Depending on when the bird was killed, what it had eaten and how old it was, the taste and texture could be unpleasant. It was even sometimes recommended by medieval cooks that peacock meat be replaced with goose and sewn up inside the skin instead. This was not to say peacock was always a dis-pleasing dish. If the peacock was young and properly prepared it could be quite tasty. Putting lard or fat under the skin ensured the bird did not dry out while being cooked. In modern experi-ments it has been found that to achieve the right flavour the bird has to be very slowly and carefully roasted, over a whole day.

Smaller households would not have had the luxury of peacock or swan. Many ate mostly domesticated fowl, goose being a common dish at Christmas as well as chicken or capon, (a castrated cockerel). These birds would simply have been roasted in their skins. There are many recipes in med-ieval texts giving directions for the preparation of fowl, par-ticularly capons, and though they were not as luxurious as those using wild birds, such dishes were by no means any less enjoy-able to eat on Christmas Day.

To accompany the meat there was stuffing. Origin-ally known as forcemeat, the term stuffing was first re-corded in English in 1538. The medieval mixture differed a little from

Like the peacock, the swan, a royal Christmas delicacy, was stuffed and presented to the table as a living bird. MS Harley 4751 f.41v. (© *The British Library*)

the modern variety. While there is a possibility that the antiseptic properties of sage, marjoram and thyme might have been helpful in offsetting the ill-effects of eating badly cooked or unwholesome poultry, there are other, better attested reasons for stuffing the bird. Trials in the Hampton Court kitchens show that filling the carcass with stuffing helps the bird stay on the long iron spit that rotated it over the fire. It was also a useful way of making the meat go further and fill up the diners, and helped the bird retain its shape during cooking.

The peacock takes pride of place at a medieval banquet. Many hours of preparation would have gone into creating a lifelike centrepiece like this. (*Getty Images*)

The Ancestors of Plum Pudding and Christmas Cake

Christmas pudding and Christmas cake have similar origins and although neither would have featured on the medieval table, the sweet dishes that did appear were the ancestors of these two seasonal treats. The one dish that could be the ancestor of both is the plum porridge, which consisted of a broth of beef or mutton, wines, spices, dried fruits with breadcrumbs to thicken it. There was also frumenty, a similar dish but made up of hulled wheat boiled in milk, with eggs, spices and sugar added. The plum porridge or frumenty was consumed on Christmas Day as a kind of preparatory lining of the stomach before the rich and fatty foodstuffs to come. Plum porridge may originally have been known by a different name as it was only in the thirteenth century that dried fruits began to arrive in England from Portugal and the eastern Mediterranean, so it was only then that dried plums (prunes) could be added to the mix.

A peasant warms his toes by the fire. From the frescoes of the Panteón Real in the basilica of San Isidoro in León, 1130. *(Imagen Mas)*

With all the fruits and breadcrumbs in the porridge it became a very thick dish. Cooks started to pour it into skins and boil it in cauldrons of water like black puddings. This made the mixture firmer and gave it a shape but it was still far removed from the modern Christmas pudding, since it still contained meat broth. This was finally removed by the Victorians, just as they had removed the meat from the mince pie. The pudding was no longer used as a light dish to line the stomach before a meal, it was a heavy and rich dish served as dessert.

Christmas cake may share its origins with the Christmas pudding. Some sources suggest that the plum porridge recipe was adapted and became a cake mixture with the addition of flour. Since this did not occur until the sixteenth century, it would seem to suggest that rich fruit cake was unknown in Britain in the Middle Ages. This is incorrect. Medieval people did enjoy rich fruit cakes, though not until the thirteenth century, when dried fruits became available. Dishes baked for special occasions, such as the Scottish Black Bun, were rich fruit cakes and there was a special custom involving the Twelfth Night Cake.

Twelfth Night is 6 January, the traditional day when all decorations should be taken down otherwise bad luck will befall the household in the coming year. It is the day on which the Church celebrates Epiphany, the arrival of the Magi at Bethlehem and thus the demonstration of Jesus to the wider world. In medieval times it was also the day when presents were exchanged. Twelfth Night involved feasting and entertainments and part of these games was the Twelfth Night Cake. This cake was baked with two objects inside it, a pea and a bean, one in each half of the cake. The cake was shared among the guests as they arrived at the festivities, men receiving slices from the right side of the cake and ladies from the left. The man who found the bean in his slice became king of the revels for that evening, and the woman who found the pea became the queen. It was sometimes the case that the recipients of the bean and pea were pre-arranged to ensure that a particular couple were put together for the night.

Twelfth Night Cake

Preheat the oven to 150°C/fan 120°C/Gas mark 2   *The mixture fills a 6 inch/15cm round cake tin*

INGREDIENTS:

170g/6oz butter
170g/6oz sugar
170g/6oz flour
½ teaspoon each:
　ground allspice
　ground cinnamon
　mace
　ground ginger
　ground coriander
　ground nutmeg
2 grinds of pepper

3 tablespoons of
　brandy
3 eggs
340g/12oz currants
42g/1½oz flaked
　almonds
28g/1oz orange and
　lemon peel finely
　chopped
1 tablespoon honey

1. Soften the butter in a mixing bowl. Add the sugar and cream together with the butter until the mixture appears light and fluffy.
2. Add the eggs one at a time beating well and also adding a tablespoon of flour to prevent curdling. Once all the eggs are mixed in add the brandy, then the flour and spices, folding them in to keep air in the mixture.
3. Finally stir in the currants, almonds, lemon and orange peel and honey.
4. Pour the mixture into the prepared cake tin. At this point you could also add a dried pea and a dried bean to the cake if you want to have a Bean King and Pea Queen ceremony. (Do <u>not</u> use a kidney bean.)
5. Cook for two hours until brown on top.

Wassail

assail was a popular Christmas drink that has its origins in pre-Christian pagan practices of tree worship. The custom continues to this day, particularly in parts of the West Country, with revellers going to orchards and pouring the alcoholic beverage over the roots of the trees, thereby hoping to ensure a good harvest in the coming year. This ancient fertility rite was widespread in the medieval period even after conversion to Christianity. It was one of the old superstitions to survive, and few landowners or farmers would forget to wassail their trees, even if they hired other people to do the task for them. This form of wassailing generally took place on Twelfth Night, but the drink itself was popular throughout Christmas.

Wassail is a brew of ale, apples (hence its strong connection to fruit trees), spices and, later on and when it was available, sugar.

Apples kept well over winter and could be turned into cider, so they were a welcome addition to this seasonal drink. Ale was drunk all year round, by all ages, even children, though there were three strengths and only

Harvesting apples. Petrus de Crescentism, *Des Profits Ruraux des Champs*, France, late fifteenth century. (*MS Royal 2 b. VII fol. 78v. © The British Library*)

Serving wassail at the Christmas feast, although these glum revellers appear to have already had their fill. Add. MS 35215, f. 97. (© *The British Library*)

the weakest was drunk daily. Being so used to ale throughout the year, it made a pleasant change to drink a different beverage and wassail was hugely popular and often drunk to excess.

'Wassail' or 'wes hal' means 'be thou hale', 'be in health' or 'be well'. The person offering the drink would offer their wishes of health to the recipient and they were expected to reply with 'drinkhail', meaning 'drink good health'. The toast 'wes hal', however, did not relate only to the drink that was named after it; the toast could be used for any alcoholic drink. Geoffrey of Monmouth, the early medieval chronicler of the Kings of Britain, writes of an incident involving the daughter of King Hengist, who presents her monarch with a cup of wine and says 'wes hal' as she does so. Perhaps this means we have confused the words a toast with an actual drink that used to be called something else. There is another piece to the puzzle. It is suggested that our word 'toast', as in raising a toast to someone, in fact derives from the practice of putting toasted bread in the wassail, the person who then received the bread being thought lucky, which is why we toast someone's health.

There was a special wassail bowl, made of wood and decorated with ribbons. This would be passed round a gathering, each person sharing a piece of the luck or health that the wassail was supposed to bestow when they drank from it. There were wassail songs to be sung with much revelry and rejoicing. Another practice was to go from house to house with a bowl of wassail, knocking at each door and offering the bowl. The householder would take a drink to bring them luck in the new year and then replenish the bowl with their own wassail before it was carried on to the next house. Some people still organise such wassail gatherings where everyone brings their own alcohol and shares it among the group. As in medieval times it is a chance to drink to excess and celebrate the ending of one year and the beginning of another.

Christmas Wassail

This recipe makes 1½ pints of wassail, enough for 6 small glasses. Adjust the quantities as required.

INGREDIENTS:

Juice and zest of 1 lemon
⅛ pint of apple juice
⅛ teaspoon of ground nutmeg
¼ teaspoon of ground ginger
¼ teaspoon ground cinnamon
28g/1oz sugar
500ml/1 pint ale
1 teaspoon of honey

1. Simmer the apple juice, lemon juice and zest, nutmeg, cinnamon, ginger and sugar in a pan, until the sugar has dissolved but ensuring the liquid does not boil.

2. Add the ale and honey and then heat through, taking care not to boil the wassail.

3. Serve warm with lemon slices floating on the top.

CHAPTER THREE

CAROLS FOR THE COMMON MAN

Carols and Hymns

What exactly is a carol and how does it differ from a hymn? Unfortunately the difference is not as clear as one might think and some Christmas songs that we refer to as carols would perhaps be better thought of as hymns. One definition has it that the hymn is a devotional song, written to be sung in Latin by the clergy and not intended to be performed by the general congregation; the carol, on the other hand, is generally written in English, or a combination of the native tongue and Latin, such as the Boar's Head carol mentioned in Chapter 2, and is often composed by a lay person. Carols also often treat their religious content in a light-hearted manner and are seasonal. Another definition concludes that carols are songs with spiritual or religious meaning, that are designed to be contemporary with their time, expressing current ideas and opinions and meant to be enjoyed by the populace, often being less complicated to sing than

Figures dancing to music played on the tabor and bagpipes. *(MS Roy 20 A SVII f.9, British Library/Bridgeman Art Library)*

their church cousins. This last definition quite clearly demonstrates the nature of the carols of the medieval period. Though Christmas hymns and poetry pre-dated the earliest ones, carols brought a new element to the celebration of Christmas. Some were bawdy and related little to the religious festival for which they were composed, while others narrated the stories of the Nativity and made them popular. The carol was another teaching tool for the medieval Church, even though many of the clergy refused to condone secular carols. It was a way of bringing the Nativity into clearer focus, and as each subsequent age incorporated new material so sometimes the subject matter of hymn and carol combined and it has become less clear where one ends and the other begins.

The Earliest Christmas Songs

The first music to celebrate Christmas did not come in the form of a carol. Christmas music started out as Latin hymns until eventually more popular and secular songs came to be written. Possibly the earliest Christmas hymn was written by St Ambrose, bishop of Milan from AD 374 to AD 397. His work was entitled 'Veni Redemptor Gentium' translated as 'Redeemer of the Nations, Come'. Like all early hymns it is completely in Latin and would therefore have been incomprehensible to most of the ordinary worshippers who heard it. It is a theological song

A fifteenth-century writer pauses for inspiration before penning the next line, from *Le Roman de la Rose*, begun by Guillaume de Lorris and finished by Jean de Muen. (© *The British Library/Heritage Image Partnership*)

designed for the clergy to sing that praises the birth of Jesus Christ, speaking of the promise of salvation the child brings. Also writing during and shortly after Ambrose's lifetime was the Christian hymn composer Aurelius Clemens Prudentius, who lived from about AD 348 to AD 413. He composed the hymn 'Corde Natus Ex Parentis' or 'Of the Father's Love Begotten', which is better known than Ambrose's hymn. Though these hymns are among the earliest western Christian music celebrating the birth of Christ, it took another saint to make Christmas music accessible to the medieval public.

The Music of Francis of Assisi

St Francis of Assisi has a strong connection to the medieval Christmas, and in many ways he made it what it is today. He was the first to create a nativity scene with a crib and a barn full of animals to watch over the baby Jesus. His role in instigating the writing and singing of carols turned the early Latin hymns into the festive music we know today.

St Francis's early life influenced him to use song as a way of teaching the secular public about Christ. Francis lived from 1181 to 1226 and spent much of his youth as a troubadour, an educated minstrel who composed poetry, often about love. By all accounts he was a man who lived life to the full and was joyful and charming, a romantic and fashionable figure in his home town of Assisi, Italy.

Francis became concerned about the wave of heresy, known as Manicheism, that was sweeping

Italy and sought to refute its denial that Jesus was God incarnate. He wanted to remind the people of Christian teaching in a way they would easily understand. Francis, along with the order of friars he founded, began writing what are thought to be the earliest true carols. They were devotional poems in the vernacular and set to popular folk music; many also included dances and were soon fulfilling Francis's mission of reminding the peasantry of the teachings of Christ. Several of the songs were performed around the nativity scene which Francis staged and were enjoyed as part of the Christmas celebrations.

It is not known how many of the carols Francis composed himself. It is widely supposed that he wrote the 'Song of Brother Sun' and that it was shortly after he completed this piece that he set his

Altar frontal, *St Francis and Scenes from his Life* by Bonaventura Berlinghieri. *(San Francesco, Pescia, Italy/Scala Archives)*

disciples the task of writing carols. Many Franciscans took up their pens, but only a few are known by name such as Jacopone or Jacoponi da Todi, who was writing at the end of the thirteenth century and composed over one hundred songs. Francis's carols started to migrate, first to Spain then to France and Germany. In 1224 the Franciscans arrived in England and set about composing new carols in English for the native population. The earliest extant English Christmas carol, 'A Child is Boren Amonges Man', is found in a set of sermon notes written by a Franciscan friar before 1350. The carol had arrived in England and a new era of music had begun.

The Middleham Jewel (reverse) showing the Nativity. This rare and beautiful piece, found in Yorkshire by metal detectorists in 1985, was probably made in London late in the fifteenth century and shows a version of the Nativity influenced by St Bridget of Sweden's vision of the birth of Christ. Several saints, including St George, are engraved on the border. (*Reproduced by permission of the Trustees of the Yorkshire Museum*)

Nativity Carols

Although the Franciscans had created carols and had brought them to England, it is generally believed that the earliest truly English carols, composed by Englishmen and specifically written to celebrate Christmas, did not appear until the fifteenth century. These were not just devotional songs written to teach people about their religion, but rather were used to express rejoicing at the nativity; eventually they strayed from the original subject matter into other areas, some of which retained pagan aspects such as the carols devoted to holly and ivy.

Unsurprisingly, what may be the oldest carol of this new wave of verse concerns the Nativity. Written around 1410 and one of the earliest to have survived, this is only a fragment and speaks of the Virgin mother singing to her baby as he lies in the cradle. It is very characteristic of its period with pronounced alliteration. A very gentle song, it portrays the Virgin as an ordinary mother singing to her child just as any medieval woman might. Expressed in the immediacy of everyday language, the song begins with 'I saw . . .', suggesting that the singer was actually an eyewitness to the event. Below, the song is presented in its original Old English with a modern translation.

> I saw a swete semly sight,
> A blisful birde, a blossum bright,
> That murnyng made and mirth of mange,
> A maydin moder, mek and myld,
> In credil kep a knaue child,
> That softly slepe; scho sat and sange.

Lullay, lullow, lully, lullay,

Bewy, bewy, lully, lully,

Bewy, lully, lullow, lully,

Lullay, baw, baw, my barne,

Slepe softly now.

Translation:

I saw a sweet seemly sight,

A blissful bird, a blossom bright,

That morning made and mirth among,

A maiden mother meek and mild,

In cradle kept a knave child,

That softly slept; she sat and sung.

Lullay, lullow, lully, lullay,

Bewy, bewy, lully, lully,

Bewy, lully, lullow, lully,

Lullay, baw, baw, my bairn,

Sleep softly now.

Many of the early nativity carols are very personal, singing not of divine beings or spiritual figures as the church songs did, but instead of ordinary people who were doing their best in a difficult time. Christ is a baby like any other, though he is often portrayed as more peaceful, perhaps more knowing, than mortal children. But his parents are common people. Take the earlier example of St Ambrose's 'Redeemer of the Nations, Come'. In his song he speaks of the salvation Christ will bring; in the early English carols little or nothing is said about what the baby Jesus will accomplish in his life, rather they sing of his birth and the Nativity.

Every aspect of the Nativity was covered in these early carols except the journey to Bethlehem itself. The Annunciation, when Mary is told by the angel Gabriel that she will give birth to the son of God, is covered in another fifteenth-century manuscript that is supposed to have belonged to a professional minstrel. The manuscript is damaged, but still

legible and the carols it contains may have been popular even before the carol of 1410. The Annunciation carol goes as follows, presented here with the original spelling and a translation.

Gabriell, that angell bryght,
Bryghter than the sonne is lyght,
Fro hevyn to erth he took hys flyght,

In Nazareth, that gret cete,
Befor a maydyn he knelyd on kne
And seyd, 'Mary, God is with the,

'Heyll, Mary, full of grace,
God is with the and euer was,
He hath in the chosyn a place.'

The Virgin Mary serenely receives the angel's message. Illumination by Jean Bourdichon of Tours, France (MS Add. 25254, *British Library/Bridgeman Art Library*)

Mari was afraid of that syght,
That cam to her with so gret lyght,
Than seyd the angel, that was so bryght,
'Be not agast of lest ne most,
In the is conseyuyd the Holy Gost,
To saue the sovles that war forlost.'

Translation from Christmas and Christmas Lore,
T.G. Crippen

Gabriel, that angel bright,
Brighter than the sun is light,
From heaven to earth he took his flight,

In Nazareth, that great city,
Before a maiden he kneeled on knee,
And said 'Mary, God is with thee,

'Hail, Mary, full of grace,
God is with thee and ever was,

He has in thee chosen a place'
Mary was afraid of that sight,
That came to her with so great light,
Then said the angel, that was so bright,

'Be not aghast, least me most,
In thee is conserved the Holy Ghost,
To save the souls that were forlost.'

Several of the fifteenth-century carols actually ask the question what an ordinary woman would do, how she would feel if a glorious angel came down from heaven and knelt before her. Mary seems more human in these carols and that would have touched the ordinary audience listening to or singing the songs. She was a person just like them.

But while the carols embraced Mary as an everyday girl who had greatness thrust upon her, the wise men or Magi were a different matter. They were exotic, coming from a far-off land, bearing

rich gifts: gold to represent Christ's kingship, frankincense to represent his godhead or godliness and myrrh to show his mortality. The men who brought these gifts were kings, sometimes named as Caspar, Melchior and Balthazar; one was young, one was old and one was of middle age. A carol that tells of the arrival of the three men and their later journey back to their homeland – in some carols referred to as India – was written by James Ryman around 1492. Below is a portion of the carol that speaks of the gifts the Magi brought.

The Dream and the Adoration of the Magi, from the *Missal of Robert of Jumièges, c.* 1016. (Bibliothèque Municipale, Rouen/Lauros/Giraudon/Bridgeman Art Library)

A sterre shone bright on Twelfthe Day,
Ouer that place where Jhesus lay.

On Twelfthe Day this sterre so clere,
Brought kinges iii oute of the eest,
Vnto that King that hath no pere,
In Betheleem Jude where he did rest.
This sterre that day tho went away,
From that swete place where Jhesus lay.

Bothe golde, encense, and swete myrre thoo,
Alle thre they gave vnto that chielde,
The whiche is God and man also,
Borne of a virgyne vndefielde.
This sterre that day tho went away,
Fro that swete place where Jhesus lay.

The Adoration of the Magi, from the *Book of Hours of Louis
d'Orleans*, 1490, by Jean Colombe. (*The National Library,
St Petersburg/Bridgeman Art Library*)

Translation from The Early English Carols, *R.L. Greene*

A star shone bright on Twelfth Day,
Over that place where Jesus lay.

On Twelfth Day this star so clear,
Brought kings three out of the east,
Unto that King that has no peer,
In Bethlehem Jew where he did rest.
This star that day though went away,
From that sweet place where Jesus lay.

Both gold, incense, and sweet myrrh though,
All three they gave unto that child,
The which is God and man also,
Born of a virgin undefiled.
This star that day though went away,
From that sweet place where Jesus lay.

Not all the carols are based on the Nativity; some pursue the later life of Christ and others relate tales of his mother and father before he was born.

Carols about the Life of Christ

The more unusual carols sung at Christmas time often referred to legends about or relate incidents from Christ's childhood, which were not always flattering to the young Saviour. The stories come from the Apocryphal Gospels, and were composed during the Middle Ages by monks for the common people who were interested to learn of the early life of their Saviour. One of the legends converted into a carol is the story of Mary and the date tree, or, after it was later confused with Eastern mythology, Mary and the cherry tree. This follows the episode of Joseph, portrayed as an old man, walking with his young wife in a cherry orchard. Every branch of every tree is laden with fruit and Mary asks her husband if he will pick her some, but Joseph has been troubled with doubts as to whether Mary's pregnancy is truly divine and refuses.

All illustrations in this section: A glum-faced group of musicians playing various medieval instruments. Add. MS 42130. *Luttrell Psalter,* f.176. (© *The British Library*)

Mary said to cherry tree, 'Bow down to my knee,
That I may gather cherries by one, two, and three,'
The uppermost bough then bowed down to her knee;
'Now you may see, Joseph, those cherries were for me.'

The actions of the trees in bending down for Mary proves to Joseph that his suspicions are unjust; he asks forgiveness and is pardoned. Later an angel comes to him and tells him that the Christ will soon be born and that his birth will take place in a stable with oxen standing round.

The cherry tree carol is an example of a divine act relating to the as yet unborn Christ. Other carols turn the young Saviour into a less than moral youth who is flawed with pride and rage, perhaps recreating him as an average person, albeit with divine powers. One such is the Withy carol, probably dating from the fifteenth century. A rather sorry episode is related in this verse when Jesus is insulted by three boys. In a fit of anger and hurt pride he creates a bridge out of sunbeams to span the ocean and proceeds to cross it, but when his tormentors follow him they fall through the bridge and are drowned. Mary punishes Jesus with a green withy – what we would now think of as a willow twig – and, filled with contempt for the plant after his beating, Christ curses the tree so that forever 'the withy shall be the very first tree that perishes at the heart'.

Compare this to a later carol also based on a gospel from the Apocrypha and you can see the contradictions. The carol of the Holy Well, though based on medieval sources, may have been written in the Tudor period. It has Jesus ask his mother if he may go and play by the holy well. She gives her permission, but when he reaches the spot the children already there, the offspring of lords and ladies, refuse to let him near and Jesus returns home. Mary learns of the event and says to her son: 'Take away those sinful souls, and plunge them deep in hell.'/'Nay, nay,' sweet Jesus mildly said, 'Nay, nay, that must not be./There are too many sinful souls crying out for the help of me.' A very different Jesus from the one that plunged three boys into the sea and let them drown.

It is difficult to know how popular the carols about Christ's life were in comparison to those about his nativity. They certainly show the different ways composers pictured the young Christ, sometimes violent and wrathful, at others forgiving and peaceable. There is one final set of carols that must be mentioned, those in which the infant Christ tells his mother of his future crucifixion. In these often touching carols Jesus comforts his weeping mother saying, 'Now peace, Mother, now peace, Mother, your weeping doth me grieve./For I must suffer this, for Adam and Eve.'

Pagan Carols

While some carols concerned themselves with the birth and life of Christ, others were about nature and the world, often incorporating older heathen traditions within the new musical type. The Boar's Head Carol mentioned earlier is an example of this. As we have noted, the tradition of the boar's head stems from the Viking custom of sacrificing a swine to their god Frey. Though the recollection of this pre-Christian association must have passed from living memory before the carol was written, it is recalled when the boar's head makes its appearance at the Christmas feast.

This is not the only example of such a carol. Several written in the fifteenth century take holly and ivy as their subject and show difinite pagan influence in their use of symbolism. These songs seem to have been used in dances where men and women faced each other and sang their own lines while dancing. The songs clearly define the differences between the sexes, holly being male and ivy female, and the ivy often getting the worst of it.

The following is a fifteenth-century carol about the holly and ivy.

Nay, Iuy, nay, hyt shal not be, iwys;
Let Holy hafe the maystry, as the maner ys.

Holy stond in the hall, fayre to behold;
Iuy stond without the dore; she ys ful sore a-cold.

Holy and hys mery men, they dawnsyn and they syng;
Iuy and hur maydenys, they wepyn and they wryng.

Ivy hath a kybe, she kaght yt with the colde;
So mot they all haf ae that with Ivy hold.

Holy hat berys as rede as any rose;
The foster, the hunters kepe hem fro the doos.

Iuy hath berys as blake as any slo;
Ther com the oule and ete hym as she goo.

Medieval musicians perform enthusiastically for the king. Perhaps they are playing a Christmas carol. (*Private Collection/Bridgeman Art Library*)

Holy hath byrdys, a ful fayre flok,

The nyghtyngale, the poppynguy, the gayntyl lauyrok.

Gode Iuy, whatt byrdys ast thou?

Non but the howlat, that kreye, 'How, how!'

Translation:

Nay, Ivy, nay, it shall not be, indeed,

Let Holly have the mastery, as the manner is.

Holly stand in the hall, fair to behold;

Ivy stand without the door, she is bitterly cold.

Holly and his merry men, they dance and they sing;

Ivy and her maidens, they weep and they wring
   [their hands].

Ivy has a chilblain, she caught it with the cold;

So may they all have always, that with Ivy hold.

Holly has berries as red as any rose;

The forester, the hunters keep them from the does.

Ivy has berries as black as any sloe;

There came the owl and ate them as she goes.

Holly has birds, a full fair flock;

The nightingale, the green woodpecker, the gentle lark.

Good Ivy, what birds have you?

None but the owlet that cry 'How, how.'

Some of the words in the carol are not easy to translate, for instance the poppynguy is usually taken to mean parrot, but here it refers to an English bird so is thought to be the woodpecker. It is immediately clear from the verses that the holly is intended to have the upper hand. He is dancing within the hall merrily while outside the ivy grows cold and ill, which may relate to an ancient custom associated with Christmas which has it that luck will only follow if a man is the first to set foot within a hall or house at the start of the new year. Women were excluded from the hall at this time until a man had entered. The verses may also refer to a type of dance in which a group of female dancers would play the ivy and would be excluded from the group representing the hall and the holly, thus they would 'stand without the hall'. These carols and dances hark back to ancient fertility rituals, thus we have the clearly defined male and female verses.

Other versions of the holly and ivy compositions take a different moral stance. In a carol from the fifteenth century the ivy is 'The most worthy she is in town', an ideal of medieval womanhood 'soft and meek in speech' and desired by all and blessed by God. As with other carols the two standpoints are very different; in one ivy is forced to stand outside in the cold and thought little of, while the other is the 'most worthy' and blessed within the town. So the pagan carols did not entirely abandon God, but they were not the church songs of their predecessors. Then again, most carols were not performed in church but were the voice of the common people: they were performed as dances, sung by mummers who journeyed from house to house collecting money or alcohol from the occupants, and functioned as entertainments and a way of learning the stories of Christ. Even though some diverged from the original carol St Francis conceived, many kept his religious message and have lasted to the present. For the medieval man and woman, as it is for us today, it just would not have been Christmas without carols.

CHAPTER FOUR

GREEN MAGIC

The Symbolism of Green

evergreens such as holly, ivy and mistletoe decked the medieval house in the bleak days of midwinter, bringing hope of renewed life to the darkest days of the year. The practice was controversial, as the Church saw many Christmas customs as pagan traditions thinly glossed with a Christian meaning. In some European countries decoration with evergreens was banned, but in England and Germany evergreen was widely used and even the later disapproval of the Puritans did not stop people from bringing greenery into their homes in winter.

The Romans used holly, ivy and mistletoe as part of their Saturnalia festival, a religious occasion marking midwinter that allowed great promiscuity, drinking, feasting and mischief, when masters exchanged places with their slaves. The Saturnalia soon became synonymous with orgies. No wonder, then, that even the medieval Church, many centuries after the Romans, disapproved of using evergreens to celebrate a Christian festival when the plants had such strong connotations of the earlier heathen customs.

In the depths of winter greenery brought hope of renewed life, although this farm has yet to be decorated. From *Les très riches heures du Duc de Berry*, by the Limbourg Brothers. *(Victoria and Albert Museum/Bridgeman Art Library)*

The Church's disapproval of winter greenery was mainly directed at mistletoe, which even until recent times was frowned upon as a church decoration, though the other pagan evergreens had gradually migrated into the building. Mistletoe was a sacred plant of the Druids, who thought it could cure any ailment. They would collect it only with the greatest of care, using a golden sickle as it was believed the magic of the plant would be destroyed if it was cut with any other metal.

Nevertheless, in the Middle Ages people still gathered the plants and adorned their homes. They respected the symbolism of the plants and much care had to be taken in bringing them into the home as well as in removing them. For instance, they could not be taken into the house before Christmas Eve, nor removed before Twelfth Night, else the good fortune they bestowed on the household would be forfeit. In some places it was considered unlucky to burn the plants once they were taken from the house – instead they had to be left to wither outside – but in others the opposite was true and they had to be burned. But nearly everywhere it was agreed that they should not be left in the house, perhaps because the Druids had taught that the plants were homes to wood spirits that could cause mischief in the household. The occupants were safe from these naughty forest sprites during the period between Christmas Eve and Twelfth Night as the power of Jesus Christ was within their home as they celebrated his birth. His strength kept the older wood spirit magic at bay. Unfortunately after Twelfth Night the sacred powers of the Christmas season vanished and the sprites were once more free to cause havoc. This strange blend of old and new beliefs was also frowned upon by the Church, yet could not be shaken from a population still steeped in superstition. To this day there are many still who feel it is bad luck to leave the Christmas decorations up after Twelfth Night.

Holly

Holly was thought to bring good luck to the home and protect it from lightning, which is why people planted holly outside their doors to protect them during thunderstorms. Holly was also believed to offer protection against witches, on account of the red of the berries, red being thought to have the power to detect evil. In the medieval period these powers of protection were said to include the detection of goblins and other evil spirits that could terrorise a household, especially young girls. It was also thought that the prickly varieties of holly were male and the smooth leaved variety female, hence they were known as he-holly and she-holly. The superstition arose that, depending on which type was first brought into the home, the plant would predict who would be the dominant figure in the coming year, either the master or mistress. Though it was known the holly had male and female varieties it was generally considered a male plant. Men would carry the berries or leaves on their person as this was thought to make them irresistible to the opposite sex. In song the holly was always male and its female equivalent was the ivy.

Holly did eventually find favour with the Church, though some of the uses of the plant were still frowned upon, such as the custom in Wales for the men and boys of a village to flog the bare arms of the women with bunches of holly until they bled. The holly lent itself easily to Christian assimilation. Some thought that it was the wood of a holly tree that was used to make the Cross for Christ's crucifixion, while the leaves were thought to have been used for his crown of thorns and it was even believed that the holly had only had yellow berries until Christ's blood was shed on the Cross, when they turned red. More importantly, the holly was connected to the Nativity, the evergreen leaves represented Jesus's eternal life while the white flowers were symbols of the Virgin's Immaculate Conception and of her milk that nourished the infant Saviour.

Ivy

Ivy was not as joyfully welcomed into the house as holly. It was usually banished to the outside, a practice reflected in many medieval holly and ivy carols where the holly holds mastery over the hall while the ivy shivers outside in the cold. Ivy was deemed feminine though how it gained this association is unclear, as it is also uncertain why holly is male; perhaps it was a folk memory of the Roman cult of Bacchus, a god of wine who wore a crown of ivy. He had a special sect of female worshippers known as Bacchae who drank an intoxicating concoction of the juice from ivy leaves

All illustrations in this section: Ivy was not always welcomed into the home. It could be associated with healing, but also conversely with death. (Bodleian Library, University of Oxford. MS Ashmole 1431 fols 25v-26r/MS Bodl.130 fol.32r)

and the toxic fly agaric mushroom. It was certainly at one time believed that ivy wood placed in a glass of wine would filter out poison. It was the knowledge of its associations with Bacchus that kept the heathen plant outside the hall while other evergreens were taken in.

The nature of the ivy was also said to be clinging and feeble, taken by some as an analogy to womanhood, but by others as an emblem of a broader human weakness that needed to cling to the strength of divine support. But because of its habit of clinging to anything, and perhaps because it was often seen in graveyards and on tombs, ivy had a darker aspect and was associated with death, so perhaps it is not surprising that a symbol for the grave and mortality should be kept at a distance when Christmas was about birth and renewal.

Ivy was not considered entirely bad, however. It was another plant believed to deter witches and when it grew on the side of a house it was thought to predict the future – for as long as it thrived everything would be well, yet should it wither disaster would strike the household. Despite its pagan past the ivy even crept into churches, perhaps not in its living form, but as carvings in stone and wood. However, it was still not a favoured plant and even though it had some healing properties the ivy only ever saw Christmas from outside, in the cold.

Mistletoe

Mistletoe has ties to both Christian and pagan legend. It was considered a 'heal-all' by the Druids, whose great reverence for it came from the fact that the plant grew off the ground, never touching it. The plant's magical properties were thought especially strong if it was found growing on an oak, which is a rare occurrence. The Druids believed that anything found growing on oak had immense healing powers and took great care when removing mistletoe from the tree, making a sacrificial offering of two white oxen before cutting the plant with a golden sickle and catching it in a cloth.

In Norse mythology mistletoe was known as the plant that caused the death of the god Balder. His mother Frigg wept for her son and her tears formed the pearly white berries of the mistletoe and she then kissed everyone who passed beneath the tree where the plant grew and commanded that whenever people met beneath the mistletoe they should do no harm to one another but kiss and go in peace. Some sources believe the custom of kissing beneath the mistletoe derives from this ancient legend and suggest that it arrived in England via the Viking invaders and became ingrained in medieval Christmas activities.

Like the other evergreens mistletoe acquired a Christian meaning in the medieval period when a new urban legend began to circulate that the wood of the cross on which Christ was crucified actually came from the mistletoe rather than the holly, the belief being that in those distant days the mistletoe had actually been a tree. It was thought that after Christ's death the mistletoe was so ashamed of

being used for the cross that it shrunk from a tree into the small plant it is today and was denied any contact with the ground. This legend has links with the myth of the death of Balder, in which the mistletoe acts as his unintentional murderer, as well as ties with the Druids' belief that mistletoe lost its magic if it was allowed to touch the ground.

This attempt to Christianise the mistletoe had little effect on the Church, the clergy forbidding use of the plant anywhere within their walls. One exception was York Minster, where every Christmas a large bunch of the evergreen plant was laid on the altar. This tradition is thought to be a throwback to the Roman Saturnalia, but is a remarkable example of a pagan custom being adopted into the Church – as we have seen, a frequent occurrence at the medieval Christmas.

Bringing Home the Evergreens by Pauline Baynes (*Illustrated London News/Bridgeman Art Library*)

For the ordinary medieval man and woman there were many reasons why mistletoe should be so favoured as a Christmas plant, not least of which was its role as a fertility symbol linked with the practice of kissing beneath it. In winter the plant was fed to the cattle to keep them healthy and ensure fertility for the coming year; women also carried sprigs of mistletoe to help them get pregnant. It was thought an antidote to any poison, as well as an aid in treating epilepsy, heart disease, nervous disorders, toothache, snake-bites and, rather oddly, was believed to help defuse quarrels, though how it achieved this is unspecified. Mistletoe, like its evergreen companions, was a deterrent to witches and protected against lightning strikes. Mistletoe's connection to lightning went further, as it was believed the plant formed when lightning struck a tree. With so many uses it is hardly surprising that mistletoe was fondly regarded by the ordinary people, especially as at Christmas it provided a licence to flirt freely with members of the opposite sex. Despite clerical disapproval, mistletoe became a firm fixture at Christmas.

The Glastonbury Thorn

The legend of the Glastonbury Thorn is one of the most unusual stories connected with Christmas and one already well known in the medieval period. It relates to a strange event that baffles scientists to this day and is witnessed every year by the inhabitants of Glastonbury. The story began just after the crucifixion of Jesus, when Joseph of

Arimathaea, the owner of the tomb where Christ lay for three days, came to England bearing a staff said to have grown from a thorn taken from the crown of thorns Christ had worn. As Joseph rested one night in Glastonbury with his weary followers he stuck the staff, which was of hawthorn, into the ground, whereupon it immediately sprouted leaves and blossom and took root. The wondrous event occurred on Christmas Day and so inspired Joseph that he decided to build a church in Glastonbury.

The miracle of the Glastonbury Thorn was repeated each year with the plant blossoming near or on Christmas Day. Cuttings were taken from the original plant and one was said to have been planted in Appleton, Cheshire by a crusader returning from the holy wars in 1125. It was reputed that this thorn also flowered at Christmas.

For centuries people witnessed the Thorn opening on the day of Christ's birth. The current Glastonbury Thorn, grown from a cutting of the original which was destroyed by the Puritans, still flowers in winter, a peculiar and rare event that is yet to be fully explained. The Glastonbury Thorn's importance was that every year the miracle happened: a tree blossoming out of season showed the power of God. Other trees supposedly bloomed on Christmas Eve, but it is only in the Glastonbury Thorn that we can still see a medieval miracle at work.

The Earliest Christmas Trees

While our modern idea of a Christmas tree adorned with glistening ornaments and standing guardian over hoards of presents did not exist in medieval Britain, the decoration and worship of trees was not uncommon. The fir tree in particular was regarded as a Christian symbol and there is a legend that refers to its spiritual significance which talks of a monk, St Wilfrid, who disliked the Druid practice of worshipping oak trees. One specific tree was a focus for the Druids and Wilfrid set out to cut it down. As he felled the oak it split and from its centre a fir grew. Wilfrid said that the fir was dedicated to Christ, its evergreen branches representing the eternal life of the Saviour. He turned the veneration of the tree to veneration of the maker of the tree and the evergreen fir became a part of the Christmas greenery, though perhaps not as popular as the holly, mistletoe or ivy. A similar eighth-century legend places the act of felling the oak in Germany and attributes it to a different English saint, Boniface.

It was also in Germany during the medieval period that the fir tree came to symbolise the Garden of Eden in mummers' plays and there is a suggestion that this also occurred in England. Even so, the fir tree was still an outside decoration; a candlelit fir was raised in a London street during the fifteenth century but there are no extant records of trees being found inside the home. Indeed, the earliest painting of a Christmas tree dates from just after the end of the medieval period, in 1521, and shows a procession winding down a German road bearing a decorated tree and followed

Possibly the earliest existing picture of a Christmas tree being paraded through the streets with a bishop figure to represent St Nicholas, 1521. (*Germanisches National Museum*)

by a man on horseback who appears to be a bishop or saint, perhaps the St Nicholas of Christmas legend. Since the painting comes near the end of the medieval period it is highly likely that the practice of carrying Christmas trees down the street was known in the Middle Ages, if not in England, certainly in Germany.

Still, a truly medieval Christmas would probably not see a fir tree inside the house. If some grew nearby they may have been decorated in remembrance of St Wilfrid's words, but it was just as likely that fruit trees or oaks would be adorned for very different, pagan reasons. The problem was that there was already an evergreen ornament to dominate and brighten the hall, one which carried the essential ingredients of the Christmas tree: candles, fruit, greenery and other decorations. This was known as the kissing bough and for many centuries it took pride of place in the home at Christmas, far longer than the comparatively recent fir.

The Kissing Bough

The kissing bough was most commonly a ball of greenery, composed of holly, bay or similar winter plants that could be obtained easily and in large quantities. Its original significance was probably to do with fertility as apples were placed inside it and beneath hung a sprig of mistletoe, which was very closely linked with fertility rites. As with most of our Christmas traditions, the bough became incorporated into Christian practice and transformed into a symbol of Christ, a crown of blessing or an image of incarnation. Overleaf are instructions for making a spherical kissing bough.

Originally the kissing bough would have had a wooden frame, probably of thin willow or hazel branches supple enough to be formed into circles. The difficulties of shaping the wood, and the fire hazards inherent in the structure, which will eventually include candles, means that wire coat-hangers or garden wire that can be formed into circles should be used. There is no limit to the size of the ornament; judge the circumference of your wire hoops by working out how large you want the final piece to be, not forgetting that mistletoe hangs down from the bottom and adds extra height to the finished bough.

The kissing bough looks spectacular hanging from the ceiling in the centre of a room and brings a touch of the medieval Christmas to a household.

The Kissing Bough

1. Shape five wire circles and fit four together vertically, starting with two fitted at right angles, wiring them together at their centres and leaving four equal quarters. Then fit the second two into the gaps, thus creating a sphere with eight equal sections. Tie the joins together with garden wire. Fit the fifth circle round the middle of the sphere horizontally and wire in place.

2. Now insert your apples. Hang them with strong cotton from the top of the sphere where the four circles meet, not too low, as they will catch on the candle, and they look better if they are nestled against the evergreens when the bough is finished. Once they are hanging where you want them, wire a candle into place inside the bottom centre of the sphere, making sure it does not sit too close to the apples.

   On larger kissing boughs candles could be placed on the horizontal middle wire in each of the eight sections, but great care must be taken with these candles as when the bough is finished it will be highly flammable and if the candles are

The Kissing Bough

too thickly encased in evergreens they could set fire to the whole structure. If candles are being used, the kissing bough should never be left unattended while alight and precautions should be taken to prevent the greenery catching fire, such as not letting the candles burn too low and keeping a jug of water on hand in case the worst happens. A safer alternative, though far from authentic, is to use electric lights and this is advisable if children are present or the bough is in a place where people could knock into it and set themselves alight, something that was not uncommon when candles were involved.

3. Next, find suitable greenery to decorate your kissing bough. Holly looks highly effective and lasts well in the house. Box is a more recent alternative, as is laurel. Mixing evergreens can be very effective, though some sources say the kissing bough should only ever have one type of evergreen. Whichever evergreen you use, wire it to the sphere covering it all but not filling in the gaps too much so that the candle and apples are visible within. Finally, wire a sprig of mistletoe underneath the bough.

CHAPTER FIVE

SEASONAL SAINTS

Martinmas

Only a few of the many saints' days in the church calendar had special significance for ordinary men and women and St Martin's Day or Martinmas was one of them. Falling on 11 November, St Martin's Day marked the beginning of winter and the start of the Christmas season. It was a time for animals to be slaughtered and their meat hung in chimneys or smokehouses to provide a supply of food for the household over the coming months. This preserved food, known as Martinmas meat, or sometimes in older spellings as Martlemas meat, would have been essential for survival through the cold winter months and probably provided a source for the Christmas feast in poorer houses.

Martinmas was also the day for paying rent or tithes, often in the form of crops or cattle. Recorded penalties from later centuries such as the confiscation of a white bull with red ears and nose for defaulting payers have a medieval ring to them, as does the practice of villagers in Warwickshire walking around a stone cross set on a hill and laying

St Martin's kindness to a beggar inspired the custom of begging on his feast day. *(Bodleian Library, University of Oxford. MS. Lat. Liturg. D. 42. fol. 35r)*

money in a hole on the cross as their St Martin's Day tithe, a practice recorded in a 1940s book on calendar customs.

Martinmas was not just about rents and slaughtering animals. It was also a feast day, a time for drinking, eating and celebration. For others it was known as Beggar's Day, when children dressed in rags went from house to house singing and asking for alms, a custom common to many feast days and derived perhaps from the giving of alms to pilgrims returning from the crusades.

With so many activities on Martinmas, St Martin himself might have become a little forgotten. He was a soldier from the fourth century AD, the son of pagan parents who placed him in the army as an officer at the age of fifteen to dissuade him from becoming a Christian monk. This did little to change his mind, and Martin became what we would term a conscientious objector. He spent time in prison for his faith and, when finally released,

he took holy orders, eventually becoming Bishop of Tours.

St Martin was most revered for an act of kindness which he performed while still a soldier. He saw a poor man without clothing begging at the gates of Amiens during a cold, harsh winter and though he had little himself he divided his cloak and gave half to the beggar, which has led to the Saint being portrayed with a partial cloak and poor men at his feet. Since he is the patron saint of beggars it is perhaps unsurprising that children should dress in rags and ask for alms on his day, or that there should also be much drinking for he is the patron saint of tavern keepers and wine growers, a useful excuse for wassail on a cold November day.

St Martin, though possessing little himself, divides his cloak with a beggar (Michelino da Besozzo, *c.* 1420). (*Pierpont Morgan Library, New York/Scala Archives*)

St Thomas's Day

St Thomas's Day fell on 21 December from the twelfth century onwards and was an occasion for celebration as it also marked the winter solstice, the point in the year when the day is at its shortest and the night at its longest. There are several saintly Thomases but the one commemorated on the 21st is the apostle, sometimes known as Didymus. Both his names mean twin and it was commonly thought that he was Jesus's brother. He was also 'doubting' Thomas.

The Incredulity of St Thomas, made for Aethelwold, Bishop of Winchester, by his chaplain Godeman, *c.* 980. (Add 49598 f.56v. *British Library/Bridgeman Art Library*)

A carpenter, Thomas was revered for his generosity and on his day it was customary to give to the poor. On this feast day it was mainly old women who walked the streets collecting alms, though children and representatives of poor families would also go begging. This practice was known as to 'go Thomasing', 'go a gooding' or 'go a corning', the latter name referring to the gathering of corn or other grains rather than money from the houses; in return the recipients of these gifts would bestow a blessing on the household or give a sprig of holly or mistletoe.

Until relatively recently schoolboys had their own customs for this day which may stem back to the late medieval period. They would race to the school house and if they reached it before the school master they would bar him from entering and burn the master's rod. Exactly how this connects to St Thomas is difficult to say, but once the tradition took root it was not easily broken.

St Stephen's Day

t Stephen, as the first martyr, earned the honour of having his feast day just after Christmas, on 26 December. In some churches it was even the custom for the deacons – whose patron saint he is – to sing an antiphon to Stephen after vespers on Christmas Day as this marked the start of his feast day.

Very little is known about Stephen other than the New Testament account of his death by stoning outside the Damascus Gate in Jerusalem. He is often portrayed with a stone on his head or holding stones in his hands, the stones often being referred

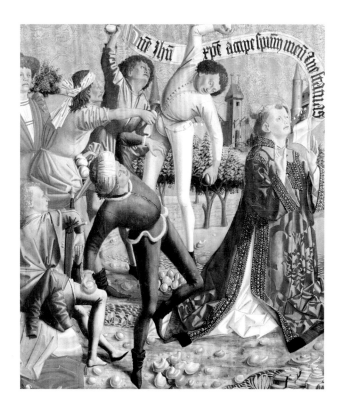

The stoning of St Stephen, from the altarpiece of St Stephen, c. 1470 by Michael Pacher. (Musée d'Art et d'Archéologie, Moulins, France/Lauros/Giraudon/Bridgeman Art Library)

A historiated initial 'S' depicting the stoning of
St Stephen. MS 572 f.32v. (Museo di San Marco
dell'Angelico, Florence/Bridgeman Art Library)

to as St Stephen's loaves. Perhaps because of his
connection with stone he is also the patron saint of
builders and bricklayers.

Despite the lack of knowledge of Stephen's life,
his feast day was vigorously celebrated as a time for
ancient superstitions and practices. It was commonly a day for mumming plays and sword dances,
as well as rather less appealing activities. For instance, it was believed that all animals that worked
hard throughout the year, particularly horses,
should be bled on St Stephen's Day to ensure
vitality and health through the coming twelve
months. The unfortunate beasts were first ridden
hard to raise a sweat and then bled. Bleeding the
horses on St Stephen's Day meant that on account
of the Christmas holiday, they would have at least
two days to recover from their ordeal before they
were put back to work.

Wren hunting was another common pursuit on
26 December and the poor birds were often stoned

to death and paraded around the streets on a pole wreathed in holly. Anyone who gave money to the hunters would receive one feather plucked from the bird which was supposed to avert shipwreck, making the custom popular with sailors and their families. In other customs the wren, sometimes called the king of the birds, was buried in a sombre funeral after being killed. The little birds suffered this sorry treatment because it was believed that St Stephen had been imprisoned before his stoning and was attempting to escape, but as he did so a little wren began to sing and unwittingly alerted the guards, who caught him for his execution. Even as late as the twentieth century the wren was made to pay for his betrayal, which is why the 26th was sometimes known as Wren Day.

There are two carols connected with St Stephen, one directly, the other indirectly. The first was written in about 1400 and, aptly enough, is entitled 'Carol for St Stephen's Day'. It portrays Stephen as a servant of Herod working in the King's kitchens and the first verse sets the scene vividly, however historically inaccurate the carol may be.

Stephen out of kitchen came, with boar's head in hand;
He saw a star was fair and bright over Bethlehem stand,
He cast down the boar's head, and went into the hall;
'I forsake thee King Herod, and thy workes all;
There is a child born in Bethlehem better than we all.'

The second carol connected to St Stephen is 'Good King Wenceslas', who looked out of his window on St Stephen's Day, but although the tune used for the carol dates back to the thirteenth century, the lyrics do not; they were composed in the nineteenth century and are supposed to relate to a true event.

Holy Innocents' Day

The 28 December is the day that commemorates the slaughter of all young boys under the age of two on the orders of King Herod. Herod had heard from the Magi that the king of the Jews had been born and he asked them to report back to him the location of the baby Jesus once they had found him. Fortunately the Magi were forewarned by an angel not to go back to Herod, who intended to kill the Christ child. Infuriated by the ruination of his plans Herod ordered the slaughter of all the infant boys in Bethlehem, in the hope that Jesus would be among them. It is this biblical story that is recalled on Holy Innocents' Day, or Childermas, and the children who lost their lives at Herod's hands have become the patron saints of foundlings.

Probably because of the cruelty and devastation that Holy Innocents' Day recalls it was not celebrated with the vigour other festivals enjoyed. It was a day of fasting instead of feasting and was considered a time of great bad luck. Any kind of work attempted on the 28th would fail, anything new started would either be destined to remain unfinished or end badly. It was also believed that on whatever day of the week the 28th fell, that same day would be deemed unlucky for the next twelve months.

Despite children being given more freedom on Holy Innocents' Day, even to the point of being allowed to play in the church, it was also customary in some parts to whip them. This was said to recall the cruelty inflicted during Herod's slaughter, but as the custom also occurred on other days in different countries, particularly St Stephen's Day in Germany when the boys whipped the girls or the servants whipped their masters, it is possible that it comes from a Roman festival, Lupercalia, where young men would run through the streets with whips with which they hit any woman they met, bestowing on them good luck as they did so. Whatever the true source of the custom, children soon learnt to rise early to avoid their elders and the whip and gradually it became tradition for the first to wake to punish with a beating those still in bed.

Other traditions on Holy Innocents' Day usually involved children. In the thirteenth century at Godstow the children said the public prayers on this day, and later the occasion developed into a procession that was only ended by Henry VIII in 1540.

Herod watches as his soldiers slaughter the innocents of Bethlehem (Giotto). *(San Francesco, Assissi, Italy/Scala Archives)*

Epiphany or Candlemas

Epiphany came on 6 January and for most people it was the end of the twelve days of Christmas and the day for taking down the decorations; it was believed that those who failed to do so would be cursed by bad luck in the coming year. Epiphany was also called Twelfth Day, not to be confused with Twelfth Night, which came, as might be expected, the day before, on the 5th, and had its own customs and traditions. Epiphany was a church festival intended to celebrate the arrival of the Magi at the crib where Jesus lay. Though in earlier days Epiphany had been combined with Christmas Day and the Nativity, by the Middle Ages it had come to be treated as a separate festival.

Special church plays were performed to re-enact the moment when the Magi arrived bearing their gifts. This play was known as the Feast of the Star. Three priests dressed as kings and with servants carrying their offerings entered the church and would act as if they had just spotted the star that would guide them to Bethlehem. This star, as recorded in accounts from Yarmouth written during the last half of the fifteenth century, was often mechanical – being moved by ropes and pulleys so that it would appear to travel down the church and lead the three Magi to the high altar. A curtain was drawn back to reveal a real child in a crib. The Magi would worship this child and offer him their gifts, after which prayers would be said. Finally, a boy dressed as an angel would appear and conclude the ceremony by telling the Magi that all the prophecies had been fulfilled.

Though Epiphany was commonly perceived as the end of Christmas there were those who argued that the actual end of the season came nearly a month later, on 2 February. This was Candlemas, an important feast which recalled the Purification of Mary after the birth of Jesus and the presentation of Jesus in the Temple, where he was acclaimed by Simeon as the 'light to lighten the Gentiles'. In some churches this then became the end of Christmas and was known as Candlemas because many candles were lit to represent the light of Jesus. Thus Candlemas was a kind of feast of light, marking the end of winter and also the conclusion of the Christmas period.

The shepherds and the Magi play their part in the Christmas story. MS 76/1362. (*Musée Condé, Chantilly, Lauros/Giraudon/Bridgeman Art Library*)

Other Saints of Christmas

Other saints whose feast days fell in the Christmas period include Thomas Becket, *c.* 1120–70, the Archbishop of Canterbury who was known in medieval times as the 'hooly blissful martir'. Murdered by four of Henry II's knights, it was only shortly after his death that his miracles began. Onlookers who had come to see the body collected blood from the ground and this was soon said to be able to cure illness. Today there is still a chapel in Canterbury Cathedral dedicated to Thomas.

Four knights overhear King Henry II's tirade against Thomas Becket, Archbishop of Canterbury, and take it upon themselves to murder him. Cotton Claudius B. II, f. 341 *Life of St Thomas Becket* by John of Salisbury, *c.* 1180s. (© *The British Library*)

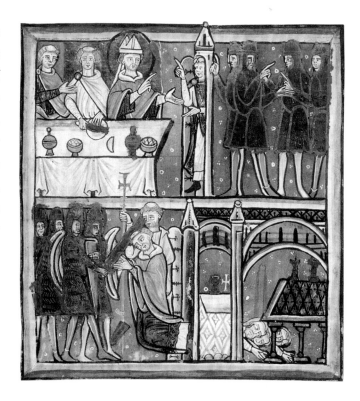

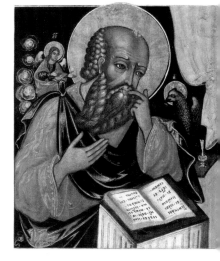

Left: St Lucy holding a candle, the symbol from which her name is derived, *lux* or light. (*Museo dell'Opera del Duomo, Prato, Italy/Scala Archives*)

Right: St John the Evangelist. (*AKG-Images/Rabatti-Domingie*)

Another Christmas figure was St Lucy, whose festival was probably linked to an original pagan celebration of light. Her origins are confused and there are many versions of her story but most commonly it is said that her eyes were plucked out when it was discovered she was a Christian and were miraculously restored by God (in other versions she plucked out her own eyes to discourage a persistent suitor). St Lucy's Day, 13 December, was a celebration of light with candles and processions. It is suggested that the festival of Christingle is a commemoration of Lucy. She is the patron saint of the blind and special guardian of girls.

St John the Evangelist had his day on 27 December. Like many feast days it was a time to drink to excess, using the weak excuse that it was in celebration of John overcoming the poison which he was forced to drink. Some sources claim that the day has its origins in a heathen wine festival, wh en magical properties were ascribed to the drink. It was supposed to make men strong and maidens fair, but in the main it was just another reason to drink the night away.

St Francis of Assisi and the Nativity

St Francis wanted everyone to be able to see and understand the wonderful thing that God had accomplished in the birth of Jesus so he presented the story of the Nativity in his unique style. In 1224 in Greccio, Italy, he decided to create a scene that depicted the Christ Child's birth. This was not the first time a crib had been set up to portray the Nativity, which had been displayed for centuries in churches. But Francis did not simply want an inanimate statue at the core of his Nativity scene, he wanted something to which the people would relate. He arranged to set the stage in a village church on Christmas Eve. His friend John Velita provided him with a manger, straw and an ox and an ass. Joseph and Mary were real people asked to play the parts and to watch over the figure of baby Jesus in his crib.

Francis's presentation of the Nativity proved a great success and the idea of the crib spread across the Christian world.

St Francis places Jesus in his crib at the first performance of the Nativity in Greccio, Italy (Giotto). *(San Francesco, Assisi, Italy/Scala Archives)*

CHAPTER SIX

SMOKING FOOLS AND BOY BISHOPS

Twelfth Night Rituals

In the Christmas calendar Twelfth Night was almost as important as Christmas Day itself, but for very different reasons. Twelfth Night had more pagan associations, and was a night for dark customs and superstitions. It was a time for wassailing, young lads going from house to house singing a drinking carol or taking the alcohol to a local orchard and bathing the trees in it to ensure a good crop the following year. It was the night when legend had it

the oxen would go down on their knees to welcome the Christ child. Some might even be heard talking in their stalls on this special night, and the bees would come buzzing out of their hives at midnight.

The medieval Twelfth Night was an exciting time of feasting and traditions. It was customary for mummers to perform plays for the wealthier households and there would be dancing and games, especially the traditional selection of the King of the Bean and Queen of the Pea involving the Twelfth

Night Cake, as described in an earlier chapter. But while the court and the larger manors were celebrating with feasting and music, the peasantry were performing their own customary rituals.

As evening approached on Twelfth Night, the medieval farmer with his farmhands and servants would prepare to enact an ancient ritual to ensure the fertility of his land for the coming year. They would go down to the fields and find the highest spot to set twelve small fires and one large bonfire going. Once the fires were lit, pledges were made with wassail and there was much shouting. It seems likely that this was an ancient custom whose origins, now lost, may lie in pre-Christian beliefs. As we have seen, the pragmatic Christian solution to all the ancient pagan customs that people insisted on

Twelfth Night saw the culmination of the Journey of the Magi. Master Berthold Sacramentary, *c.* 1200–32. (*Pierpont Morgan Library, New York/Scala Archives*)

celebrating was to adapt them and give them new meaning, so the Twelfth Night fires were dedicated to Jesus and his twelve Apostles, the largest fire representing Jesus and the fire that was symbolic of Judas being stamped out as soon as it was lit.

Twelfth Night Cake has already been discussed, but in that example it was used in the grand manor houses and in the royal courts. The peasantry had their own cake and, as might be expected, it was associated with farming superstitions. The Twelfth Night Cake that would be prepared in the farmhouse was baked with a hole in the centre and this was important as, after setting the bonfires in the fields, the farmer and his servants would head for the barn where the oxen were stalled. Just as the fields had been toasted with fire and the trees wassailed, so the oxen needed to be safeguarded against ill-luck in the coming year and their fertility and vitality ensured. For these reasons the medieval farmer had his Twelfth Night Cake ritual. He chose his best ox and placed the cake on one of the horns, hence the hole. The ox would try to toss off the strange object that had suddenly been placed on its head. The gathered company watched eagerly to see where the cake would land after the ox had managed to shake it loose from its horn. If it fell behind the animal it was called the Istress and belonged to the wife of the farmer; if it fell in front it was called the Boosey and belonged to the master. It is at this point that the ceremony ended and the cake was taken back inside to be eaten.

A medieval depiction of bees flying in and out of a hive from a bestiary or moralised history, Latin, Durham, 1200–10. Roy 12 C XIX f.45. (*British Library/Bridgeman Art Library*)

Boy Bishops

The custom of the boy bishop seems an unusual one in the light of the Church's general disapproval of other Christmas traditions, particularly since in many ways the function of the boy bishop appears far more blasphemous than placing a piece of holly or – worse – mistletoe in the church. But the custom prevailed throughout the thirteenth and fourteenth centuries, only to die out with the Tudors as both Henry VIII and Elizabeth I banned the custom, though only the latter was successful in stopping it for any length of time.

The boy bishop was chosen from among the choristers of the cathedrals. He was dressed in full episcopal garb, suited to his size, with mitre and crozier and his term began on 6 December, the feast of St Nicholas, patron saint of children. Other sources suggest the tradition derived from the Roman Saturnalia when it was customary for both sexes and all ranks to switch roles, the master becoming the slave, men becoming women. Perhaps the role reversal is a distant memory of this.

Whether it was to show reverence to a saint or as the re-enactment of a pagan role reversal, the term of the boy bishop was a very serious business. From 6 to 28 December, Holy Innocents' Day, the boy bishop performed all the functions of a priest. He took all the services apart from the Mass, appointed canons to attend him from among his fellow choristers and was treated as a real bishop. If he died while in office he was buried with the full honours of a bishop – such a case is commemorated in Salisbury Cathedral, where a statue has been found of a young boy dressed in the full regalia of a bishop. Originally thought to have been an exceptionally small grown man, it was finally realised that the sculpture actually represented a boy bishop.

The boy bishops were not without some adult guidance. Early in the thirteenth century it became customary for the cathedral dignitaries to act as subordinates to their young bishop, becoming taper or incense bearers. It seems that this was considered one step too far in the reversals of roles and the action was banned in 1263. But generally the public and particularly royalty approved of the boy bishops. King Edward I had vespers sung to him by the boy bishop and his canons in December 1299 and rewarded the choir grandly with 40s. Later Edward III also had a service performed for him by the boy bishops, but seems to have been less impressed as he only saw fit to reward them with 19s and 6d.

Unfortunately, later authorities seem to have taken a dim view of the proceedings, comparing them to the riotous Feast of Fools or Feast of the Ass. They claimed that the boy bishops created disorder in the churches and made a mockery of church ceremonies. Perhaps some of the criticisms stem from what happened after the services, when the boy bishop and his entourage would tour the local houses not begging for alms but rather demanding them as of right because of their priestly status. It would appear that if there was any trouble it was caused by the public who attended the boy bishop's services and a statute was passed that anyone throwing things at, or causing disruption to, the boy bishop could be punished.

The Lord of Misrule and the Feast of Fools

Christmas seems to have provided the opportunity for many instances of the inversion of normal rules and customs. These customs were Roman in origin, but they enjoyed a strong revival in England during the medieval period and were at their height in the fifteenth century, before being steadily condemned and eventually forbidden.

The Lord of Misrule started out as a respectable role within the household and royal courts and usually entailed the steward or the household's fool or jester being chosen to play the part over Christmas. He was expected to order the Christmas festivities, watch over the other servants and entertainments and generally ensure that everything went smoothly. In wealthy homes and colleges the Lord of Misrule was a welcome sight at Christmas and was paid well for his efforts. He was also known in the Church and was sometimes referred to as the Abbot of Misrule whose function was similar to that of his lay counterpart, although among the clergy the role became confused with the Feast of Fools, a much less respectable celebration.

In fact it did not take long for the role of the Lord of Misrule, which for many years had been becoming increasingly disreputable, to descend into an excuse for rough and destructive behaviour. It was the practice in certain parts for a crowd to gather and appoint a Lord of Misrule from among their number. They would then march with their new leader towards the church, playing pipes, banging drums and cavorting in the style of mummers with masks. Upon entering the church they would disrupt whatever service was in progress with dancing, singing and shouting.

Bedfellow to the Lord of Misrule was the dubious Feast of Fools. It seems to have begun in the eleventh century and is therefore probably older than the tradition of the Lord of Misrule, who may have derived some of his functions from this strange celebration when the church was turned upside down. The Feast of Fools began on New Year's Eve when, after vespers and at the words of the Magnificat 'He has put down the mighty from their seats and exalted the humble' the precentor, who oversaw the ordering of the services, handed his staff to a subordinate chosen as lord of the feast. It was from here that the feast descended into chaos.

The church was turned topsy-turvy with the motion of handing over the precentor's staff. Dice were cast on the altar with the priests standing by, while others ate black pudding off it. Absurd songs were sung in deliberate disharmony and old leather

Courtly figures dancing in a genteel fashion, unlike their peasant counterparts who danced in church, from the *Roman du Saint Graal*. MS 527 fol. 1r. (*Bibliothèque Municipale, Dijon/ Giraudon/Bridgeman Art Library*)

was burnt in mockery of incense. Some clergy wore monstrous disguises and danced in the choir and all was turned to blasphemous disruption condoned by the church. Is it any wonder, then, that the common people thought it only fair that they should have their own version of the Feast of Fools, choosing their own Lord of Misrule and causing confusion at religious services? Ironically, they were condemned as troublemakers.

One last tradition of the Feast of Fools, which gives it the name of the Feast of the Ass, was to bring a donkey into the church and to sing Latin hymns to it, in which the refrain was an imitation of the beast's braying.

From the regions of the east,
Came this strong and handsome beast:
None with Donkey may compare,
For the loads that he will bear,
Hail, Sir Donkey, hail!

This custom appears to have originated in France and was supposed to represent the Flight into Egypt. In certain parts of the country a girl rode the donkey with a baby in her arms, but mainly it was the animal alone that was brought into the church. This was one of the many dubious acts that eventually brought the Feast of Fools into disrepute and saw its banishment. Other crimes had the lord of the feast drenched in bucketfuls of water or riding through the town in a carriage while behind him his clergy came with a cart of dung which they proceeded to throw at the spectators who had gathered to watch the procession. Despite all this, the Feast of Fools survived the medieval period and really only vanished completely under the iron will of Cromwell and his Puritans.

The Yule Log

The tradition of the Yule log stems from the Vikings and their midwinter celebrations. In the cold climate endured by northern European societies it was not only essential to have a good source of heat and warmth, but it was also necessary to perform rituals that would appease the god Thor and welcome back the sun, ensuring that the harsh winter came to an end. There was a special time to perform the rites and this was Yuletide, which lasted twelve days and was the source of the twelve days of Christmas. The Yule log was an integral part of the Yuletide ceremony. The log had to burn for the whole length of Yuletide to guarantee the sun's return and, more

Bringing in the Yule log with much rejoicing. (*The Story of Christmas*, Michael Harrison)

Alcohol was sprinkled on the Yule log to welcome it into the house. (*The Story of Christmas*, Michael Harrison)

practically, to ensure that the inhabitants did not have to go back out into the bleak snows of winter to gather more fuel. It was very important that everyone who was able helped to bring in the Yule log, as all who did so would be protected from witchcraft in the coming year, a major concern to the Vikings and to medieval people.

The log had to be welcomed into the assembled company, so was doused in alcohol, which ensured it caught fire faster, and was carefully positioned in the hearth – not too close to the centre, where it would burn too quickly, nor too far away, where it might go out. It was vital that the log did not burn away before the twelve days were over and that the flames did not go out as this would spell disaster for the people who had brought it in. The log was lit with a piece of wood from the previous year's Yule log and tended attentively through the next twelve days. It was an art to keep the log burning for the full Yuletide, but the Vikings saw this as a necessary act to ensure a good coming year.

Raiding, and some-times trading, through-out Europe, the Vikings brought the traditions of the Yule log with them. The societies they invaded adopted the practice but since they were mostly Christian, they changed its meaning. No longer was it a ritual to honour Thor but instead came to symbolise the need to keep the Christ child warm in his stable over winter. It developed into an important part of the medieval Christmas, albeit one still hedged about with pagan superstitions. A common tradition was that unless the servants, particularly the maids, washed their hands before touching the log it would burn dully; in other places it was thought a person with a squint or anyone who entered the hall barefoot while the log was burning would bring ill luck with them. A similar superstition is reflected in the custom of first footing, mentioned below.

When the log had burnt for the full Yuletide, people collected the embers of the fire, just as the Vikings would have done, as these ashes were believed to have special properties. It was thought that if they were kept in the house they would act as a talisman against lightning strikes and the outbreak of fire. They were also believed to cure toothache, rid cattle of vermin and act as a useful fertiliser for the fields. To throw the ashes out on Christmas Day was tantamount to blasphemy as it was thought to be throwing them right into the Saviour's face.

As hearths decreased in size so the Yule log lost its meaning. Smaller versions were sometimes adopted but they did not have the grandeur of the original custom and of course could not last for twelve days so the time they should burn was shortened to twelve hours instead.

Christmas Games

During the medieval period part of the excitement of the season was the opportunity to play games and to gamble, for adults as well as children. For some this was the only time of the year when they could play dice or games of chance, while those who would perhaps not do so during the rest of the year might indulge at Christmas. But something that everyone enjoyed were the large group games, which usually resulted in the players looking foolish but provided great mirth for the assembled company. Such games can still be played today as part of a medieval Christmas re-enactment, but care should be taken with certain games that can be hazardous.

Playing a Christmas favourite, Blind Man's Buff. (*Stowe MS. 955 f. 7. © The British Library*)

Hoodman Blind, or Blind Man's Buff

A person is nominated and blindfolded. He or she is then pushed and buffeted by the other players until they manage to catch someone; this done, the person caught is then blindfolded in their place. In medieval times the original game was known as Hoodman Blind because the person nominated was blindfolded with their own hood reversed on their head. In certain manuscript drawings it appears that the other contestants then used their hoods to strike at the blinded player and attempt to avoid capture.

An initial letter with a snap-dragon ready to play his game. (*The Book of Days*, vol. 2, R. Chambers)

Snap-dragon

This is a more dangerous game that had to be played with care. The original version involved placing a large amount of dried fruit, such as currants, in a bowl and covering them with sufficient brandy so that the fruit would float. The brandy was then set alight and the players had to snatch a piece of fruit from the bowl and eat it as quickly as possible. The result was scorched fingers and burnt mouths hence the game cannot be recommended in its original form. Nor can its variant, snap-apple, where an apple was suspended on one end of a stick with a thread, while on the other hung a candle. The whole contraption was hung from a beam and a player would attempt to take a bite from the apple without burning their face on the candle, an almost impossible endeavour. Both these games were played with all other candles in the hall extinguished so the only light came from the lit brandy or the candle on the string, which lent an eerie atmosphere to the sport. To play snap-dragon at a modern recreation of a medieval Christmas it is not advised to use flaming brandy. Iced water makes a good substitute, and if the water is cold enough with plenty of ice cubes, pinching currants would be just as uncomfortable.

Oranges and Lemons

This game revolves around the nursery rhyme of the same name:

> Oranges and lemons say the bells of St Clements,
> You owe me five farthings say the bells of St Martins,
> When will you pay me say the bells of Old Bailey,
> When I grow rich say the bells of Shoreditch,
> When will that be say the bells of Stepney,
> I do not know says the great bell of Bow,
> Here comes a candle to light you to bed,
> And here comes a chopper to chop off your head.

The rhyme has a confused history but the game was relatively straightforward. The rhyme was actually used to select participants for a game of tug of war. Two team leaders would be chosen and they would form an arch with their arms. All the other players were supposed to march through the arch while the song was sung. As the last line was said the arms were brought down to capture the player who was passing beneath. They were then allocated to one of the teams and the game continued until all the players had been assigned to a team whereupon the tug of war could begin.

Haxey Hood game

Playing oranges and lemons would also be a suitable way to choose the teams for the Haxey Hood game. This thirteenth-century game began in the village of Haxey, Lincolnshire. The story goes that Lady Mowbray, a local aristocrat, was either riding to or riding away from the Epiphany church service when her hood was caught up by a gust of wind and blown across a field. Thirteen young men from the village were passing and saw the hood blowing away. Believing that whoever retrieved the hood would probably be well rewarded, the men all ran for the hood and fought over it until one took possession of it and raced with it towards Lady Mowbray. She was highly amused by the scene and awarded the village of Haxey a piece of land, known as the Hoodlands, with only one condition, that every year the men of the village would re-enact the chasing of her hood.

Since that day the tradition has been maintained. The residents of Haxey still gather on 6 January (Epiphany) and prepare to fight for the hood. The yearly event soon expanded from its original thirteen contestants to involve nearly all the men of the village and usually their wives and sweethearts as well. There were two teams and two goals – nowadays two pubs – but the medieval players would have had similar stopping points. The players were dressed in red and were known as Boggans. With them came the Fool and before the game could begin he would stand on a mounting block to announce the rules of the game. It was then customary to place straw around the bottom of the block and set it alight so as to 'smoke the Fool'. To some this suggests that the game has its roots in pagan times and invokes old rituals of human sacrifice, but it may also have simply been a bit of sport with everyone watching to see how long the Fool could endure the choking smoke.

After the poor Fool had been smoked the game began. A hood was flung into the air and all the players would race to get hold of it. There would then be much pushing, shoving and brawling as each team tried to get the hood back to its own point of safety. The struggle could take hours and, considering how violent some medieval games could become, football being a good example with players even dying sometimes, it is not hard to believe that people would have been hurt, maybe even seriously injured during this game. If you want to play the Haxey Hood game, you could of course go to Lincolnshire on 6 January and watch the real thing, otherwise simply arrange two teams and play a toned-down version of the sport using a cloth sack or something similar for the hood. It is not advised that anyone should be smoked as the Fool and rules should be laid down to ensure no one gets hurt.

A fool and his dog. The fool was smoked as part of the Haxey Hood game. From *La Bible Hystorians on les Histoires Escolastres*, MS Royal, E.VII, f. 241. *(AKG-Images/British Library)*

Divination, the Return of the Dead and First-Footing

Although Christmas was celebrated as a time of rebirth, there was a much more sinister side to winter and particularly to the twelve days of Christmas. As we have seen, traditionally it was a time of magic and a great many seasonal customs show this. It was the time of year when fairies, witches and goblins could roam free and in many places in Europe it was also supposed that at this time the dead would return and inspect their old homes. The belief was so strong that on Christmas Day, before the family went to church, the house was thoroughly cleaned and a meal set for the spirit visitors who would enter the house while the family was at the service and examine it, making sure it was in good order and possibly even taking a meal or sleeping in the beds. If the returning dead were pleased, the year would be prosperous and good for the family.

Other tales of the dead at Christmas probably stem from the howling winds that spring up during winter and can sound not only violent and fierce but also like the wailing voices of the condemned. Fears roused by these ghostly noises developed into tales of 'The Wild Hunt' or 'The Devil and his Dandy Dogs' or 'The Raging Host'. These were the lost souls, the unbaptised, the murdered and the suicides who were forced to roam the earth as part of a demonic hunt bringing ill luck and doom to all whom they encountered.

There were, of course, other forms of magic at Christmas and these did not involve the return of dead relatives. The festive season was a popular

Christ, God the Father
and St Thomas, altarpiece
by Konrad Witz, *c.* 1450
(see page 106).
(Kunstmuseum,
Basel/Giraudon Swiss/
Bridgeman Art Library)

time for divination, the most common reason being the desire of young girls and women to find out the name of their future husband. All manner of objects were used, even in later periods the Bible, but, perhaps because of their availability, it was the basic foodstuffs that were most frequently employed.

One method of divination required an unmarried girl to bake a cake on Christmas Eve and set it on the hearthstone with her initials marked on the surface. It was imperative that the kitchen door be left open so that at midnight the spirit double of her future beau might enter by it and prick his initials next to hers. Another form of divination was specific to the eve of St Thomas's Day. A girl would stick pins into an onion and recite a poem that asked St Thomas to grant her visions of her husband-to-be. This done, she would put the onion under her pillow and that night she would dream of her lover. If a girl was not interested in her future bridegroom's name but simply in whether she would get married at all, it was customary for her to go down to the hen house on Christmas Eve and knock at the door. If the cock crowed, it was a sign that wedding bells would ring out before the end of the coming year, but if a hen answered, the girl could be looking at a lifetime as a spinster!

To predict things other than marriage prospects different tools were required. For instance, the ivy leaf was useful for divining a person's future health. The leaf had to be immersed in a covered bowl full of water at night on New Year's Eve and left there until 5 January. It was then inspected and the condition of the leaf dictated what the next year held in store. A leaf that was still as green and fresh as the day it had been put in the water signified good health to come, but a leaf that had withered or was covered in black spots predicted ill health.

A weather prediction could be attained without the need of any object. It was thought that the weather on the twelve days from 25 December to

5 January foretold the future outlook for the next twelve months. So the weather on Christ-mas Day would mimic the weather conditions of the month of January. The weather conditions of St Stephen's Day, 26 December, predicted the weather in February, those on 27 December predicted March's wea-ther, those prevailing on 28 December pre-dicted conditions for April, and so on.

Though divination was an enjoyable pastime and perhaps brought comfort (or despair) to the med-ieval man or woman who was afraid of what life had in store for them, it was only a diversion. One of the most important customs of the season was that of the First Foot or the Letting in of Christmas, a custom that seems to have ancient origins and one that is still practised by many today as part of the New Year's fest-ivities, particularly in the north of England where it has always been popular. The superstition relates to the first person to enter a house (now translated to midnight on New Year's

Dancing was one of the many activities on offer at Christmas, as these courtiers are happy to demonstrate. From *Le Roman de la Rose*, illuminated by the Master of the Prayer Books of Bruges, *c.* 1500. *(British Library/Bridgeman Art Library)*

Eve). The first person to set foot in the hall on Christmas morning must be a dark-haired man, preferably a stranger as this is luckiest; but as dark-haired passing strangers are unlikely to arrive at the right moment a suitable member of the household was usually chosen or, among the peasantry, one man would be nominated and would visit every home in a village or settlement.

The first-footer could never be a woman, nor a fair-haired man (except in some rare cases where he must be fair), nor flat-footed. These customs are reminiscent of the Yule log tradition where people with the wrong colour hair or bare feet could not come into the presence of the log for fear of ruining its magic. It was the same with the first-footers: the wrong person entering could ruin the following year's luck. There have been suggestions that the choice of hair colour recalls a racial memory of the fair-haired Saxons driving out the dark-haired Celts, making it more propitious for a dark-haired stranger of Celtic descent to enter a house rather than a fair-haired man who might be related to the Saxons. This seems a little unlikely, especially as red-haired men were also excluded, probably because of the tradition that Judas Iscariot had red hair, making it unlucky for a man with similar colouring to be the first to enter the hall.

Christmas was a season for festivities, but also for dark superstitions and strange magic. A lot of these customs we no longer understand or care to explore, but they were an essential part of the medieval Christmas. Perhaps some were more pagan than Christian, but they all evoked that magical aura of unreality that characterises Christmas. Maybe it is time we recaptured some of these lost traditions.

CHAPTER SEVEN

St Nicholas, the Medieval Father Christmas

There is one figure who sums up the Christmas season and is recognisable to almost every child around the world. Father Christmas, or Santa Claus, is one of the strongest images of Christmas and it would be easy to consider him a relatively modern invention. Indeed, in many respects the fat, jolly man who looks like a kindly grandfather is a myth of the nineteenth century. But Father Christmas existed long before the first Christmas card depicted him, though in his earlier guises he was just as likely to have been feared by children as loved.

The Father Christmas of the medieval period may have had a Norse antecedent and had links with Odin, the Viking god who rode through the sky on the eight-legged horse Sleipnir delivering rewards to the good and punishment to those guilty of evil. But Odin had a less welcome side for he was also the bringer of winter. Travelling with him was the Dark Helper, who would later reappear when Father Christmas was reincarnated as St Nicholas. The Dark Helper was a horned creature, a demon whose sole purpose was to punish the wrong-doers. This dual nature is the source of the Father Christmas tradition; it was the prototype that would draw to itself the legends of St Nicholas.

Odin may have been preceded by a more primitive version of Father Christmas, shamanic and ancient. There is little evidence for this other than supposition, though possibly there was some worship of an Old Man Winter, as was later seen in European cultures. If we take Odin as their source we can see the foundations of modern traditions, but he was not long in his role before the rise of Christianity changed the pagan beliefs of a generous god who rode the skies rewarding the good. His successor was a wealthy bishop who gave his riches in secret to those who needed them and from the story of his various miracles the idea of Father Christmas developed. It was this Father Christmas who performed in mummer's plays and was the subject of a fifteenth-century carol that began 'Hail Father Christmas, Hail to thee'. Odin had been replaced by the true Christmas saint, Nicholas.

A Byzantine enamel of St Nicholas. (*Museo Lazaro Galdiano, Madrid, Spain/Bridgeman Art Library*)

St Nicholas, Bishop of Myra

Nicholas lived in the fourth century AD. He is thought to have been born in ancient Lycia, the modern Turkish seaport of Patara, late in the third century and legends say that from the start he was a very pious baby, standing up in his bath on the first day and abstaining from suckling at his mother's breast save for Wednesdays and Fridays, when he would only suck once. His parents were devout Christians, but also very wealthy. When they died, Nicholas was still only a young man and was left with great riches that he did not know what to do with. He decided he would give away his money wherever he saw there was a need for it.

The devout Nicholas attended church every day and as a result became bishop of Myra. The old bishop had died and the church council decreed that the first person to walk into the church the next day would be appointed bishop. It was of course Nicholas who walked through the doors first and so he became bishop, a post he held until his death on 6 December in about AD 326.

During his lifetime Nicholas performed many miracles and has become the patron saint of many different groups of people. Sailors pray to him when their ships are in danger because of legends that he saved the lives of seamen during violent storms. It is recorded that prior to his invasion of England and when his fleet was caught in a terrible storm, the Norman conqueror, William, prayed to St Nicholas and he and his ships were thus saved. Itinerant merchants, too, took him as their patron and slowly he became the protector of all engaged in long and dangerous journeys, particularly pilgrims. Nicholas is also the patron of the poor and humble, of unmarried girls, prostitutes, pawnbrokers and children.

Despite all his tireless work to help the less fortunate, Nicholas would probably have been little known outside his own country had it not been for a band of Norman pirates who stole his remains from Myra on 9 May 1087 and translated them to Bari, Italy. The justification for this raid was that the relics of the saint had to be saved from the advancing Muslims who threatened Myra. More likely it was because Bari needed saintly relics to encourage pilgrims, a big business in the medieval world, and Nicholas would not be the first saint whose bones were removed for burial elsewhere as part of a business enterprise.

The Miracle of the Two Boys in a Barrel

Nicholas became the patron saint and protector of children as a result of one of his miracles. The story goes as follows. Two young boys were on a journey to Athens, where they were to be educated, and en route had been instructed by their father to visit Bishop Nicholas to receive his blessing. They arrived at night in Myra and feeling it was too late to go to the church they sought shelter, intending to visit Nicholas in the morning. They took lodgings at an inn, but were unaware that their host had noticed their belongings and baggage and had already decided to rob the two lads in what he supposed would be an easy crime.

During the night, as the boys slept, the innkeeper entered their room and murdered them. Then, to cover his crime, he proceeded to dismember the

In this illustration St Nicholas rescues three boys from the brine barrel rather than the more usual two. (*Bodleian Library, University of Oxford. MS. Lat. Liturg. D. 42. fol. 39r*)

bodies and cut them into small pieces. To complete the grisly task the man threw the cut up corpses into barrels full of brine intending to sell the boys' flesh as salted pork and so profit further from his wickedness.

There are two versions of how Nicholas discovered the heinous act. The more miraculous method tells how he had a vision that very night as he slept in which he witnessed the evil deed. The second, less magical version, relates that he learnt that two boys were due to visit him and when they failed to appear he went in search of them. Coming to the inn he enquired if the boys had stayed there; the innkeeper, afraid he had been discovered, lied and said the boys had been there but had since left. Nicholas was unconvinced and explored the inn, finding the brine barrels. At this point the innkeeper must have been feeling very guilty and knew he was about to be found out by the bishop, so he confessed and begged forgiveness. Nicholas was moved by the man's confession and his apparent repentance. He prayed for the man to be pardoned and for life to be restored to the innocent boys. As he finished the words of his prayer the many parts in the brine barrels joined together and the two boys sprang out of the salty water and landed at Nicholas's feet. The bishop pulled them up, told them that they had God alone to thank for their lives and then with a few words of advice (possibly about dubious innkeepers), he restored their belongings to them and set them safely on their way to Athens.

It was Nicholas's remarkable act of restoring dead children to life that made him so apt a protector and friend to the young and innocent. On his feast day, 6 December, it was customary for a boy bishop to be chosen and this custom is sometimes linked to Nicholas's revival of the dead children and his status as guardian of the very young, particularly of boys.

Miracle of the Poor Girls

The miracle that truly turned Nicholas into Father Christmas involved a poor man and his three daughters. The family had fallen on hard times and could no longer afford food or clothing, let alone the dowries the girls would need to find husbands. Nicholas was passing the poor man's house one night when he heard the lamenting of the father and his children as they discussed their terrible situation. Immediately, he decided to help them, knowing he only had three bags of gold remaining from the considerable fortune his parents had left him.

Later that night he crept back to the poor man's house and went to the window of the eldest girl's room. Since it was summer the window was open and Nicholas was able to toss inside one bag of gold, which landed in the girl's stocking hanging up

St Nicholas provides dowries for three poor girls, by Ambrogio Lorenzetti, 1327–32. (*AKG-Images/Rabatti-Domingie*)

by the fireplace. The money was a welcome sight for the impoverished family and now the eldest girl had a dowry she was soon married.

The time now came for the middle daughter to be married and again the problem of a dowry arose. Nicholas returned to the house and once again threw a bag of gold through the girl's bedroom window. She too rejoiced on finding the money and was soon married. All this had come about without anyone knowing the identity of their generous patron, but the father's curiosity was now roused. He suspected that now the youngest girl needed a dowry their benefactor would return and deposit money in her room, so he lay in wait to see who would come.

As expected, Nicholas arrived one night with a bag of gold. The father watched as Nicholas approached the youngest girl's room wondering how he would get the money in, as the winter had come and it was no longer possible for the windows to remain open at night. Nicholas realised he had a problem, but swiftly solved it by climbing on to the roof and dropped the money down the chimney instead. The bag fell down and landed in a stocking just as before and Nicholas began to sneak away, his work done. Yet the father was greatly anxious to thank this strange young man who so generously gave his fortune to them. He did not understand the reason behind the gifts and was probably a touch concerned about this stranger who visited his daughters in the night. He ran after Nicholas and catching up with him spun him round. Instantly he recognised the young man and fell to his knees begging to know why such a generous servant of God would hide his deeds. But Nicholas wanted no praise for his kindness and persuaded the man to tell no one and only to be glad that his daughters would now be well looked after.

It is not difficult to see how the St Nicholas story provided material for the Father Christmas legends.

First and foremost, he is the secret provider of gifts. He comes at night, not wanting to be seen, and delivering presents to those who deserve them. If caught, he begs not to be revealed and for his kindness to continue to be secret. Are these not characteristics of Santa Claus? Medieval people also attributed gift giving and secrecy to their Father Christmas, and copied him by giving one another gifts, not on Christmas Day as has now become the practice, but on 6 December, Nicholas's feast day. There is another element to the story that reminds us of our own Father Christmas: Nicholas not only threw the money into the girl's stockings, but even delivered his final bag of gold down the chimney. While these are probably later embellishments to the story, they do appear in most versions and there is no reason to think they are not fairly old additions, perhaps even dating from the medieval period.

Even the more disreputable elements of medieval society took Nicholas to their hearts. He was the patron saint of prostitutes, and thieves were known as St Nicholas's clerks because of a reproach he had once made to a gang of robbers who promptly returned their stolen goods and mended their ways. It is not surprising, then, that three bags of gold, a symbol of giving, became associated with pawnbrokers. In the Middle Ages Lombard Street was home to many pawnbrokers and when they sought a symbol to represent their trade, they took inspiration from a statue on top of the Church of St Nicholas in Lombard Street – and the statue held three bags of gold. From then on all the pawnbrokers in Lombard Street used three gold bags or balls as their symbol and the custom has stuck to this day.

Overleaf: The polyptych of the Dominicans by Fra Angelico, 1437, showing St Nicholas of Bari, second from left. (*Galleria Nazionale, Perugia, Italy/Scala Archives*)

St Nicholas and the Dark Helper

The medieval version of Father Christmas was saintly and good and brought the deserving rewards, but what should be done with the undeserving? Just as the Church taught that the good went to heaven and sinners to hell, so it should be with Father Christmas: if he rewarded the good then the bad must be punished. But at the same time Father Christmas was based on a saint who had been more interested in forgiveness than punishment. The solution came from the Viking gift-bringer, the god Odin. He had his servant, the Dark Helper (or Dark Pete), who punished the wicked, and so now St Nicholas was furnished with the Dark Helper to work at his side.

The Church disapproved of this pagan demon walking alongside a saint and through their protests caused the Dark Helper to become chained to St Nicholas so turning him into the saint's slave or servant. But they could not get rid of the demon entirely. He was a strange creature who differed from country to country but was for the most part bestial, covered in a shaggy skin with horns and usually painted black. He carried a birch rod or whip to threaten the naughty, particularly children or women. He was usually kept in line by his saintly master, who would allow him to terrorise the children and then restrained him before he could do any real harm. St Nicholas and his Dark Helper took part in many rituals to discover who had been bad and who had been good. In some places the children were asked questions on religion and the right answers averted punishment. Even stranger customs saw Nicholas's path being cleared by ghostly creatures who lashed about with whips while behind him came a man carrying a goat's head. The head was taken through the villages and bleated outside the door of a sinner, who would then be pulled out and beaten. While adults no doubt appreciated that this was for the most part a game, children would have found it a hugely frightening experience with

St Nicholas enthroned, late thirteenth century. He was never depicted with his Dark Helper. *(San Nicola, Scandriglia, Italy/Scala Archives)*

the strangely clad and threatening Dark Helper chasing them with his rod or whip. No doubt it was thought to go some way to encourage children to behave.

There are many names for the Dark Helper; in the German Tyrol he was known as Klaubauf and in other Germanic countries Krampus, Pelz Nickel or Knecht Ruprechte. The most interesting Dark Helper was Old Nick himself. Fortunately the Dark Helper was not the only figure to appear with St Nicholas; occasionally he was replaced by St Peter, the archangel Gabriel or even Jesus himself.

St Nicholas was only one aspect of Christmas. He played a major role but he was accompanied by many other customs and traditions, games, carols and celebrations. Nor was he the only saint to figure in the season, though he is the only one who was a direct participant rather than just an influence. Along with all the other Christmas activities he made the dark winter fly by.

Bibliography

Unless otherwise stated, place of publication is London.

Alexander, Marc, *A Companion to the Folklore, Myths and Customs of Britain*, Stroud, Sutton, 2002

Baker, Margaret, *Christmas Customs and Folklore: A 'Discovering' Guide to Seasonal Rites*, Prince's Risborough, Shire Publications, 1968

Banham, Debby, *Food and Drink in Anglo-Saxon England*, Stroud, Tempus, 2004

Beckett, Sister Wendy, *Sister Wendy's Book of Saints*, Dorling Kindersley, 1998

Blackburn, Bonnie and Holford-Strevens, Leofranc, *The Oxford Book of Days*, Oxford, Oxford University Press, 2000

Bolgna, Ferdinando, *Early Italian Painting, Romanesque and Medieval*, Van Nostrand, 1963

Bord, Janet and Bord, Colin, *Ancient Mysteries of Britain*, Diamond Books, 1991

Brasch, R., *Christmas Customs and Traditions: Why We Do What at Christmas*, Angus & Robertson, 1994

Brice, Douglas, *The Folk Carol of England*, Herbert Jenkins, 1967

Brody, Alan, *The English Mummers and their Plays*, Routledge & Kegan Paul, 1970

Byrne, Lavinia, *The Life and Wisdom of Francis of Assisi*, Hodder & Stoughton, 1998

Chambers, E.K., *The Mediaeval Stage, Volume I*, Oxford, Oxford University Press, 1925

Chambers, R., *The Book of Days, A Miscellany of Popular Antiquities in Connection with the Calendar, Volume I*, London and Edinburgh, W. & R. Chambers, 1862

——, *The Book of Days, A Miscellany of Popular Antiquities in Connection with the Calendar, Volume II*, London and Edinburgh, W. & R. Chambers, 1864

Cosman, Madeleine Pelner, *Medieval Holidays and Festivals, A Calendar of Celebrations*, Piatkus, 1984

Coss, Peter, *The Lady in Medieval England 1000–1500*, Stroud, Sutton, 2000

Count, Earl W., *4,000 Years of Christmas*, Rider, 1953

Crippen, T.G., *Christmas and Christmas Lore*, Edinburgh, Blackie, 1923

Dearmer P., Williams R.V. and Shaw, M. (eds), *The Oxford Book of Carols*, Oxford, Oxford University Press, 1950

Duncan, Thomas G., *Late Medieval English Lyrics and Carols 1400–1530*, Penguin, 2000

Early Medieval Illuminations, Twenty One Colour Plates, Iris Colour Books, Batsford, 1951

Enders, Jody, *Death by Drama and other Medieval Urban Legends*, University of Chicago Press, Chicago, 2002

Friar, Stephen, *The Companion to the English Parish Church*, Stroud, Sutton, 1996

Golby, J.M. and Purdue, A.W., *The Making of the Modern Christmas*, Stroud, Sutton, 1986

Greene, R.L., *The Early English Carols*, Oxford, Oxford University Press, 1935

Hallam, Elizabeth, *Chronicles of the Age of Chivalry: The Plantagenet Dynasty from 1216 to 1377*, Tiger Books International, 1995

——, *The Plantagenet Chronicles*, Tiger Books International, 1995

Harding, Patrick, *The Xmas Files, Facts Behind the Myths and Magic of Christmas*, Metro, 2003

Harrison, Michael, *The Story of Christmas*, Odhams Press, 1951

Helm, Alex, *The English Mummer's Play*, Woodbridge, Boydell & Brewer, 1981

Heritage of Britain Reader's Digest Association, 1975

Herrin, Judith (ed.), *A Medieval Miscellany*, Weidenfeld & Nicolson (facsimile edn), 1999

Hole, Christina, *Christmas and its Customs*, Richard Bell, 1942

Hone, William, *Ancient Mysteries Described*, Ward Lock, 1970

Humfrey, Peter, *Lorenzo Lotto*, New Haven and London, Yale University Press, 1997

Knowles, David, *Saints and Scholars, Twenty-five Medieval Portraits*, Cambridge, Cambridge University Press, 1962

Le Jacques, Goff (ed.), *The Medieval World*, Parkgate, 1997

Lloyd, Christopher, *Fra Angelico*, Phaidon, 1979

Miller, Daniel (ed.), *Unwrapping Christmas*, Oxford, Clarendon Press, 1993

Morris, Desmond, *Christmas Watching*, Jonathan Cape, 1992

Orchard, Andy, *Cassell's Dictionary of Norse Myth and Legend*, Cassell, 2002

Perez-Higuera, Teresa, *Medieval Calendars*, Weidenfeld & Nicolson, 1998

Pollard, Alfred W., *English Miracle Plays, Moralities and Interludes*, Oxford, Clarendon Press, 1923

Purvis J.S. (ed.), *The York Cycle of Mystery Plays*, SPCK, 1951

Reeves, Compton, *Pleasures and Pastimes in Medieval England*, Stroud, Sutton, 1995

Renterghem, Tony Van, *When Santa was a Shaman*, St Paul, MN, Llewellyn, 1995

Roud, Steve, *The Penguin Guide the the Superstitions of Britain and Ireland*, Penguin, 2003

Sansom, William, *Christmas*, Weidenfeld & Nicolson, 1968

Simpson, James A., *All About Christmas*, Glasgow, Gordon Wright, 1994

Southworth, John, *Fools and Jesters at the English Court*, Stroud, Sutton, 2003

Strutt, Joseph, *Strutt's Sports and Pastimes of the People of England*, Bath, Firecrest, 1969

Tannahill, Reay, *Food in History*, Eyre Methuen, 1973

Waters, Colin, *A Dictionary of Saints Days, Fasts, Feasts and Festivals*, Berkshire, Countryside Books, 2003

Whistler, Laurence, *The Kissing Bough*, William Heinemann, 1953

Wilson, Constance Anne, *Food and Drink in Britain*, Constable, 1973

Wright, A.R., *British Calendar Customs, England Volume II*, published for the Folklore Society, 1940

——, *British Calendar Customs, England Volume III*, published for the Folklore Society, 1940